SOUTHERN QUILTS: A NEW VIEW

SOUTHERN QUILTS: A NEW VIEW
Bets Ramsey and Gail Andrews Trechsel

EPM Publications
McLean, Virginia

Library of Congress Cataloging-in-Publication Data

Ramsey, Bets, 1923–
    Southern quilts : a new view / Bets Ramsey and Gail Andrews
Trechsel.
       p. cm.
    Includes bibliographical references.
    ISBN 0-939009-52-8
    1. Quilts—Southern States—History—20th century. 2. Fiberwork—
Southern States—History—20th century. 3. Quiltmakers—Southern
States—Biography. I. Trechsel, Gail Andrews. II. Title.
NK9112.R37 1991
746.3975'09'049—dc20

                                 91-425
                                 CIP

EPM Publications, Inc., 1003 Turkey Run Road
  McLean, VA 22101

Cover and book design by Tom Huestis

Photographs of Exhibition Quilts by Alex Hughes

The cover photograph is a detail of "Parallelogram Diptych"
by Ellen Azhorec

Contents

Foreword

The idea for *Southern Quilts: A New View* began to form in our minds when Gail Trechsel and I were attending an exhibition, *The Art Quilt*, in Huntsville, Alabama. Organized by Penny McMorris and Michael Kile, it encompassed works especially prepared for the exhibition by selected artists who had chosen the quilt as their form of expression.

Gail, in Alabama, and I, in Tennessee, had spent several years documenting antique textiles, but seeing the contemporary quilts brought us forward to our own time and particular interests. It seemed to us that quilt artists in the southeastern United States, being widely scattered, had little opportunity to show their art in a gathering with their peers. Perhaps the cultural patterns of the South set a somewhat different atmosphere for work, and we were curious to see how they affected the artists. The traditions transmitted through generations and a general conservatism were bound to have some bearing on the work.

We spent a year gathering slides and information about quiltmakers in the South before selecting 28 artists to participate in the proposed exhibition, to be called *Southern Quilts: A New View*. All 28 accepted the challenge, and, by the following year, the majority were able to present pieces made expressly for the showing.

Only two qualifications were given to the artists. First, the piece had to be layered, with a top, middle, and a back, and fastened together in some way. Second, there was no limitation on the materials to be incorporated in the work or its format. We wanted the artists to be totally free to explore their forms in whatever direction they chose, and we were pleased to find, at the end, that they did.

We are indebted to the artists who so imaginatively fulfilled our expectations. Even before our project had fully begun, we were asked by Sandra Blain to prepare an exhibition of contemporary quilts for the gallery of the

Arrowmont School of Arts and Crafts in Gatlinburg. The school's reputation as a showcase for the nation's best artists assured us of an auspicious beginning.

We appreciate the enthusiasm of the other institutions who placed *Southern Quilts: A New View* on their schedules. Above all, we are grateful for the incredible support of the Hunter Museum of Art in Chattanooga and its unfailing staff, especially Cleve Scarborough, Ellen Simak, Jacqui Casey, and Shelia Newby. Without the museum's sponsorship, the exhibition would not have been possible.

We are especially grateful to Alex Hughes for the care he gave to photographing these exhibition quilts and to Ellen Zahorec for assisting; to Bradley Burns who photographed and installed many of my previous quilt exhibitions at the Hunter Museum of Art; to David Luttrell who photographed *The Quilts of Tennessee*; to T. Fred Miller, photographer, who shared my early quilt research; and to the institutions which graciously provided photographs: the Birmingham Museum of Art, the Birmingham Public Library, the Charleston Museum, the DAR Museum, and the Hunter Museum of Art.

Special thanks go to Michael Lassen of the Wilson Arts Center, Rochester, New York and Mary Hujsak, Librarian, American Craft Council for research assistance; to Linda Bennett who assisted with the manuscript; to Linda Claussen for being there when needed; to Dot Moye for advice; to Merikay Waldvogel for the many adventures we had studying and exhibiting quilts of the South; and to Evelyn Metzger who believed in our commitment.

Our final thanks go to Paul Ramsey and Haydn, Julia, and Andrew Trechsel for their support and cooperation.

Bets Ramsey

Tree of Life, *center medallion with borders,*
appliqued with fine buttonhole stitch, by Martha Hobbs
Lucas, c. 1790–1800 at Merryoaks Plantation,
Brunswick County, Virginia. This is a summer spread
and therefore unquilted.
(Collection of the Birmingham Museum of Art, Birmingham, Alabama;
gift of Mrs. William J. Hagan III in memory of Louise Warten Hagan,
William James Hagan, Jr., and William James Hagan III)

The Traditions
by
Bets Ramsey

Quilts, once thought of as solely bedcovers, now have uses that are limited only by imagination. Even while science and industry are changing traditional concepts of fiber and fabric, an exceptional renewal of interest in quilts, needlework, and other textile arts and their history has been occurring in the 20th century.

Domestic sewing machine purchased by the John Blair family of Roane County, Tennessee, in 1878, coming by riverboat from Richmond, Virginia. The five Blair women did weaving and sewing for members of the community.
(Photograph by Bets Ramsey, courtesy of Mary Browning)

When the loom and needle were dominant features in most households and were necessarily employed to produce domestic textiles and clothing, the mechanical sewing machine brought welcome relief. Some suggested that it was an invention of temptation and provided an opportunity to squander the resulting idle hours. Even with the machine's lightening of the arduous work of sewing all textile items by hand, women continued to do needlework for enjoyment and for family provision. When wars and economic changes caused the majority of women to enter the work force, patterns of living changed. Domestic duties and responsibilities shifted when women were no longer bound to the home, and manufactured items replaced those that had once been sewn by hand.

The period of needlework and craft exploration which followed World War II had evolved from the 19th-century Arts and Crafts movement in England, tempered by the Colonial Revival in America and the Bauhaus ideals originating in Germany. Thus the stage was set for new interpretations of material and design in quiltmaking.

A change in the quilt's form and function, from household object to work of art, has now created a need for a fresh appraisal of the quiltmaker's intentions. In order to place these new quilts of the South in proper prespective, it may be helpful to examine some of the sources from which they come.

The Atlantic seacoast of North America, south of the Potomac River, was settled primarily by colonists of English and French origin who brought with them their respective styles and traditions. Naturally they retained the European models they had known but, of necessity, modified and adapted them to the circumstances of the New World. Although an independent spirit in political matters spread rapidly, fashions and furnishings continued to be influenced from abroad.

English needle arts, practiced in professional guilds, were developed, refined, and flourished in the Middle Ages, reaching their height in the 1400s and 1500s with the exquisite *opus anglicanum*, ecclesiastical embroidery. In addition to church embroideries, bed hangings received elaborate treatment of the needle and were recorded in numerous wills of the period. Sometimes these documents even included brief descriptions of embroidery threads, techniques, and motifs. To include mention of the elegant bed furnishings in legal papers indicates how highly they were regarded.

With the Reformation, domestic and amateur embroidery flourished, aided by the publication of pattern books throughout Europe, and the ecclesiastical embroidery of the professional guilds declined. In addition to bed hangings, there were embroidered table carpets, cushions, and panels worked by women in all levels of society. Mary, Queen of Scots, was taught to embroider by her mother-in-law, Catherine d'Medici, in France, and Elizabeth I made gifts of her own handwork. She sent Henry IV of France a scarf she had embroidered and asked him to overlook its imperfections.

English needlework of the 1600s and 1700s, during and following the reign of Elizabeth, was an almost excessive part of fashion. Without going to distant museums, it is possible to experience the richness of Elizabethan dress merely by studying reproductions of the period's portraiture. Tunics, gowns, caps, petticoats, gloves, and virtually any items of adornment were lavishly decorated with embroidery and set off with lace. Complete sets of bed and window hangings and bedcovers received similar ornamentation and featured floral, Biblical, Oriental, and mythological subjects in their design.

Decorative quilting of garments was used in the mid-17th century, and by its end ornamental quilting was widely featured on beddings. Designs were worked on silk in a running-stitch, but on linen, however, a back-stitch was used to achieve a clearer line. Sometimes soft threads were stuffed into the channels of quilting to raise the pattern.

Then followed a period when Oriental design was in vogue in Europe. The style was reflected in many of the embroidered bedcovers that imitated the Chinese preference for a large central motif surrounded by wide borders. The medallion-type quilts made in America later in the century can be traced to this Chinese source of design, which was transposed to English quilts. The upper class had elaborate bed furnishings, and similar types of work were modified for the less wealthy. Servants employed in the great houses emulated, in more modest materials, the styles they had seen there.

Framed medallion quilt, a favorite style of English quiltmakers, made by Rebecca Ellen Davenport Blackwell at Clifton Farms, Fauquier County, Virginia, c. 1820–1830.
(Courtesy of the National Society Daughters of the American Revolution Museum, Washington, DC; given in memory of Nannil Levell Blackwell by Lucy Steptoe Jones)

Gradually, by the 1800s, the use of quilting decreased in English fashion and furnishings, except in the northern counties where quilting continued to be practiced.

By the time of the American Revolution, patchwork and applique had somewhat

Rose quilt, detail, made on the Hughes plantation
near Calhoun, Georgia, 1848. Mrs. Hughes and some of
her slaves did the fine stipple quilting in rows one-
fourth inch apart and heavily stuffed the roses.
(Photography by T. Fred Miller)

The Alabama Gunboat Quilt *made by Martha Jane Hatter Bullock, c. 1861, Greensboro, Hale County, Alabama.*
(Collection of the Birmingham Museum of Art, Birmingham, Alabama; museum purchase with partial funds from The Quilt Conservancy)

replaced embroidery as the popular needlework of Europe. Because of demand, wood-block and copper-plate printed fabrics were produced specifically for quiltmaking. Sewing accessories abounded. The time had come when cloth was being produced in such quantities that it was readily obtainable and inexpensive. For this reason one could afford to cut it up and sew it back together by piecing or patching.

The quiltmakers of southern France, in the 17th century, had a somewhat different approach to their work. In Provence there was a flourishing quilting industry, which may have been introduced at an earlier date through connections with Italy. There are in existence exquisite whitework quilts made in Sicily in the 15th century, and it is likely that the style was carried to southern France and readily adopted by regional needlewomen. The majority of their quilts are made from wholecloth white silk or linen, finely quilted, with stuffing and cording inserted into the quilted motifs to make a raised design. Some fewer quilts were made of other materials: colored fabric, wool fabric, or prints from India and France.

Marseilles was an international seaport and, among other things, shipped quilts from the area to England. The white quilts found an appreciative clientele there and came to be known as Marseilles quilts, named for the city of their export.

English manufacture excelled in weaving, and by mid-18th-century inventors had developed a draw-loom process of layered weaving that successfully imitated the Marseilles quilts. Although they were often identified by the same name, or as Bolton quilts, since they were manufactured at Bolton, they are more accurately called spreads because no quilting is required in their making. When the jacquard loom replaced the draw-loom in the 19th century, the same type of spread continued to be produced, even into the 20th century.

These, then, were some of the models that served the women who came to America. If they were wives of the crown's representatives, undoubtedly they brought fine treasures with them or set about to replace what they had left behind. If they were of a lower social status, they depended upon improvisation. In any case, the styles that were carried to a new land influenced fashion for an extended period, lagging behind changing modes abroad. A similar occurrence happened in Australia among the wives of the government officials who were sent to colonize the continent. They did the English-type needlework and quiltmaking they had been taught at home and followed the styles they remembered long after fashion changed in Europe.

Contrary to the writings of certain early 20th-century quilt historians, the first colonists did not commence making quilts of crazy-patch construction upon arrival to this continent. In actuality, the crazy quilt was a product of the last quarter of the 19th century. There were, however, wool blankets manufactured in quantity in English mills and available at reasonable cost. There were coverlets of various types and woven and hooked bed ruggs with heavy shag surface. According to diaries, household inventories, and wills studied more recently by quilt scholars, quilts made up a small fraction of colonial household bed furnishings. It is apparent that those recorded were considered items of luxury, not utility, and were found in the homes of the affluent.

Newcomers to the southern coastal area acquired large tracts of land on which they produced profitable crops, especially rice and indigo. It did not take long for a prosperous upper class to establish itself. With sufficient access to commercial seaports, the planters were able to export their goods and obtain

Slater Mill, the first cotton mill in the United States, Pawtucket, Rhode Island, built in 1790.

imports for their households. Not the least of these items was fabric for furnishings and apparel. With no American industry yet developed to supply fabric, the homemaker was dependent upon imported cloth or home-weaving until such time as domestic manufacture was well enough established, in the late 1700s, to begin to meet demands.

Few textiles from the 1600s exist in America to serve as comparisons to their counterparts abroad. Later examples indicate fashion followed that of Europe, perhaps with a lag of ten or 20 years. Early quilts of American origin were wholecloth quilts made of glazed wool, imported chintz, palampores from India, and wood-block and copper-plate prints. Indigo resist-dyed linen,* an early product of American textile manufacture, was eagerly adopted by colonists who wished to demonstrate their independence from England by using domestic cloth.

Resist dyeing is accomplished by applying a solution to fabric in a design pattern to prevent dye from reaching the fibers. The untreated areas will absorb the dye and become the predominant design.

Some bedcovers representative of the Revolutionary period do exist in museums and private collections. The Tree of Life, either as a block-printed or painted wholecloth piece or as an applique motif, appears frequently as the design element. Eager to please their foreign buyers, the Indian producers achieved success by adapting European-style embroidery patterns for their fabric designs. The smaller patterns in chintz and calico were equally well received by needlewomen. These fabrics from India, and those of English and French manufacture, were used for many of the quilts made along the southern coast, even as late as the Civil War.

Tree of Life, *chintz applique cut from many different fabrics, with wide chintz border.*
(Courtesy of The Charleston Museum, Charleston, South Carolina)

After the invention of the cotton gin in 1793, southern planters intensified their production of cotton. According to David Brion Davis the result was a shift in the Negro population, formerly concentrated in New England, and the eastern and upper southern states. At the same time there was increased importation of African slaves to southern ports.

Bales of cotton awaiting shipment at the South Commercial Wharf, Charleston, South Carolina.

The management of a plantation became an increasingly complicated responsibility for a plantation owner. In his absence, when he was attending to business or political matters, the mistress of the plantation would be required to make decisions, execute her husband's orders, solve problems, arbitrate disorder, and run her own household. Seldom was she educated or prepared to be an executive officer.

It is a delightful fantasy to imagine a lovely lady in fashionable gown peacefully putting in the thousands of stitches required to make an oversized chintz-work quilt for a high tester bed. If such a picture were true, she would be blessed with perfectly trained servants and slaves who could butcher, gather, preserve, store, prepare, and serve meals for the master's household; to provide clothing, food, and

medical attention for dozens of his workers; and to see to the laundry, mending, spinning, weaving, sewing, cleaning, and child-care in the big house. Perhaps there were some quiet moments for quilting. Perhaps other family members helped make the quilt. Perhaps some of the helpers were the slaves in her house.

While quiltmaking was not known in Africa, certain skills associated with it were practiced there. Stitching, applique, and quilting had been used in various ways and the techniques were carried to America to be easily incorporated in the making of bedcovers. Those skills were employed in the slave quarters as well as in the master's house. Some black quiltmakers were taught to sew within their own family circle. Some were taught by their mistresses, but not all mistresses were talented with a needle, by any means.

It is difficult to determine whether a quilt was actually made by slave labor unless there is some supporting evidence. Family tradition may or may not provide reliable information. Occasionally initials or signatures are discovered which can verify the attribution. Diaries and journals, such as the one kept by Narcissa L. Erwin Black of McNairy County, Tennessee, help identify the makers of pre-Civil War quilts when the quilts can be matched to the journal entries. Regional documentation efforts and diligent research are helping form a more coherent body of quilt history.

The state quilt survey projects, which are adding valuable information to the history of quiltmaking, began in Kentucky in 1981. More and more Kentucky-made quilts were being carried away to northern antique galleries, and a group of quilt enthusiasts determined to preserve something of their quilt heritage while they still could. The Kentucky Quilt Project was devised and, with the assistance of dozens of volunteers from the Kentucky Heritage Quilt Society, completed a survey of approximately 1,000 quilts within a year's time. Their findings were presented in a significant exhibition and book. Their contribution to recorded quilt history has provided a model for other state and regional groups to follow.

One of their findings is of particular interest in demonstrating the value placed upon fabric in the 18th century. One of the oldest quilts examined during the survey points up a common domestic practice of the period, that of recycling material. A *toile de Jouy* printed fabric from the late 1700s, titled "Penn's Treaty with the Indians," and once a set of parlor curtains, comprises the top of the quilt. The back is handspun linen, woven by the maker while she was still living in New Jersey and may have been a bedsheet originally. After she moved to Kentucky in the early 1800s, Sarah Runyan Anderson used the cloth she had saved to make into a quilt. Because of scarcity and cost, such was the regard given to cloth, and its usefulness was extended in every possible way.

Research in South Carolina has broadened the knowledge of quiltmaking as it relates to regional history. It is not unexpected to find that the framed medallion quilt was highly favored in the Charleston area, which had close European connections through the shipping trade. The style and fabrics correspond to fashions of the countries sending goods to America. Splendid examples of chintz-work are preserved in South Carolina museums and historic houses, and more were discovered through the quilt documentation days connected with the state survey of quilts. Eventually the use of the medallion format diminished as the repeat-block design became popular.

The seaports along the eastern coast provided much of the trade for developing regions of the South, with overland routes from Philadelphia and New England serving to a lesser degree. Areas inland were connected by large and small rivers affording trade by boat to centers of commerce. The ports of Mobile and New Orleans allowed access to trade from the North, from Europe, and even from the Orient. Supplies for domestic sewing were always included with other items transported for sale.

Cotton bales and dock workers on the levee at New Orleans, Louisiana.

Lucy Virginia French, of McMinnville, Tennessee, noted in her diary that her husband had purchased plum-colored silk satin for the making of a floral-embroidered quilt when he was in New Orleans. Later, in 1859, it won the maker several awards, and still later it covered the family silver and her as she lay in bed, feigning illness during a Yankee raid. It was expected that business excursions such as those made by Mr. French included shopping for items not otherwise easily obtained.

A comparable quilt was made by Martha Jane Hatter of Greensboro, Alabama, and was donated to raise funds for the purchase of a gunboat to defend the city of Mobile during the Civil War. No doubt the quilt's fabric came from a source similar to that of Mrs. French's quilt.

Laurel Horton described the availability of material for quilters of a remote mountainous county prior to the Civil War in an essay entitled "Nineteenth Century Quilts: Macon County, North Carolina." The Cherokees who built villages in the area connected their towns by a network of trails and trade routes in all directions. Early white traders followed the trails to bring tools, guns, fabric, and other trade items to exchange for furs.

Soon after the Cherokees ceded a section of land to the state of North Carolina, in 1817–19, two white settlers, Jacob Siler and William Brittain, bought an Indian cabin and opened a store. They were limited to selling or trading goods brought by wagon or horseback across the mountains from lowland cities.

As their farms flourished in the fertile valley, the early settlers extended their own trade area, delivering their products beyond the mountains to the south and east, even though a trip to market by oxcart required days of slow travel. Before long, the children of the prospering landowners were attending boarding schools in distant cities and becoming aware of fashion in architecture, clothing, and domestic arts.

Laurel Horton says that the middle-class families of Macon County raised sheep, had looms and spinning wheels, and could produce their own furnishings and everyday clothing. Woven wool blankets were practical articles which did not take long to weave, compared to making a quilt. A quilt was not regarded as an ordinary item. It took planning and effort to make a quilt, so it was likely that some expense was given to the purchase of the material. Manufactured fabrics were available locally for those who could afford them.

People of the southern mountains have been pictured inaccurately as poor, isolated, and uneducated; but Horton contends there was never a period when they were cut off from "the outside world." The quilts that were made in the mountains in the 19th century are similar in style and fabric to the quilts made in other parts of the country. Even the first settlers who followed the Indian trails were supplied by entrepreneurial traders. The trails soon became paths, then roads, and finally, highways.

A Rose of Sharon quilt from this region is typical of certain quilts made before the Civil War. Large floral applique blocks form the top, surrounded by a chintz border, a very thin layer of cotton filler finely quilted, all of a square and generous size. According to family tradition, the quilt was made by "Aunt Matt" Anderson, a live-in seamstress who was hired in the fall and winter by Dr. and Mrs. A. C. Brabson to sew for their family of 11 children. They lived in a large frame house in the Riverside community south of Franklin, in Macon County, North Carolina. It is obvious that the making of the quilt required considerable investment of time and money. The family has always regarded it as an important object.

The Civil War had a devastating effect upon the South. Many areas were heavily plundered or damaged. Some people lost everything they owned and had few resources to begin again. Families were broken, manpower lost. The economy was in a shambles. It was a harsh and bitter time, and it took years of recovery to compensate for the losses encountered.

Many of the black people who were in slavery had a difficult time becoming established as free citizens. While some were able to acquire land and become plantation owners themselves, others remained close to their former surroundings and worked for wages or shares. The story of one woman illustrates the transitional period. Granny Drummond (her first name has been lost to family members) was born and raised in slavery in Alabama and managed to keep her seven children together with her, unlike many women, until Emancipation. After receiving her freedom she moved to the plantation of Lena Blake, near Wehadkee, Alabama, where she was employed for a number of years, even while her own family increased to 16. From Mrs. Blake she learned all aspects of housekeeping and sewing, excelling most as a seamstress and quiltmaker. In her late years she joined one of her sons, a widower, to help rear his six young children. She passed on her sewing skills to her granddaughters who produced many outstanding quilts throughout their lifetimes.

Improvisation has always had a useful place in the making of quilts. Altering a pattern to fit fabric supply, incorporating extra blocks and borders to increase size, or just using scraps in an inventive way have been hallmarks of good quilt designers. This was especially true of southern quiltmakers during and following the Civil War when fabric was particularly scarce and difficult to acquire, when means were exceedingly limited. For many, it became standard practice to use only materials at hand—scraps, leftovers, salvaged pieces of garments, remnants, and home-dyed muslin—since purchasing material was impossible. Habits acquired during those periods of scarcity and economic depression were long-lasting. Even today some quiltmakers who can afford to buy new material prefer to mix and jumble their fabrics in the way to which they are accustomed

As the South recovered from the effects of the Civil War, gradual changes occurred. The agrarian society experienced encroachment by manufacture and industry, particularly in the textile field. Cotton production increased; mills prospered as they spun thread, wove cloth, printed and finished fabric; and employment rose. It is true that some of the products were not as fine as certain pre-war manufacture, but the single-color resist-prints that were inexpensively produced allowed for a dramatic reduction in the cost of material. Now and then, every

quiltmaker could afford to buy new fabric and even purchase batting. Quiltmaking flourished.

Where river transportation and Indian trails had once been the only means of travel, greater access came to the rest of the country with the development of the railroads. Mail service became more frequent. Letters and packages were no longer such a rarity. Changes were taking place everywhere, but, in the South, they were more gradual than elsewhere.

The South remained an agricultural economy until well into the 20th century. Rice and indigo had been replaced by cotton and foodstuffs as the major sources of income. Eventually land depletion and the boll weevil reduced cotton production and profits and, coinciding with the availability of factory work, led to heavy migration to cities. In the last part of the 19th century, however, before that occurrence, the land was populated by hundreds of farming families who had developed the skills and resources to be virtually self-sufficient.

Elizabeth Borders and James Madison Miller are representative of the type of farming couple found in north Georgia in the 1870s. When they married in 1873, her parents' wedding gift was a 50-acre farm six miles from Calhoun, the Gordon County seat. Her father, Andrew Borders, was a hardworking cotton farmer who believed in investing his profits in land, which he passed on to his children.

Mat worked his land well, clearing timber to increase cotton acreage and, on several occasions, purchasing adjoining property to enlarge his farm. The land provided them abundantly with food for table and livestock. Household goods and clothing were made from wool and cotton grown on the place, with the cotton crop being the main source of income.

Elizabeth's quiltmaking activities have been described by the author in an essay, "Cotton

Rose of Sharon *appliqued block quilt made by Matt Anderson for Dr. and Mrs. A. C. Brabson of Macon County, North Carolina, c. 1860.*
(Courtesy of the Hunter Museum of Art, Chattanooga, Tennessee)

Broken Stone, *scrap quilt made by Elizabeth Borders*
Miller, Redbud, Gordon County, Georgia, c. 1900.
(Courtesy of the Hunter Museum of Art, Chattanooga, Tennessee)

Country: Redbud, Georgia 1873–1907.'' The neighborhood store at Redbud served as the social center of the crossroads community. There one could buy seed, fertilizer, foodstuffs, cooking utensils, farm implements, and sewing supplies. The bolts of cloth for dresses and quilts were not replaced until they sold out but, even with this limitation, quiltmakers did not hesitate to make their purchases. There was not always time for a trip to town.

As Betty's family grew to nine members, her abilities as a manager of time and labor increased correspondingly. After daily and seasonal chores were done, she found time for spinning and weaving towels, blankets, cloth for garments, and yarn for knitting socks. Her favorite task, however, was quiltmaking.

During a winter in Georgia, 20 or more quilts were required for all the beds. Betty and her girls made warm everyday quilts for winter, some of light weight for spring and fall, and a few special ones to display when company came. Then there were quilts to prepare for future marriages. Each daughter made several tops to quilt when she became engaged, and four quilts apiece were put away for the boys when they married.

Every year when the fall crop of cotton was taken to the gin at the crossroads, a portion was set aside for family use. At home it was spun into thread and carded into batts for filling the quilts made that season. During the winter months there was always a quilt in the quilting frame, ready to be worked on during any spare moments. Sewing baskets were filled with quilt scraps and blocks being readied for more tops. It was a pleasant reward to spend a little time sewing after finishing the morning work.

Although some of Betty's household goods were handwoven, her all-purpose fabric was muslin, bleached and unbleached. It was used for sheets, pillowcases, undergarments, quilt backs, and sometimes, the tops. It washed

Loaded cotton wagon at Hunt's gin, Redbud, Georgia, in the 1970s, the last of 16 gins once operating in Gordon County.
(Photograph by T. Fred Miller)

well, was easy to sew, and took dye evenly if coloring was desired. Dyeing in an outdoor iron wash kettle was done with natural materials or purchased dyes.

Adding colored plain materials to her scraps was Betty's way of producing handsome quilts of her own ingenuity. She used the leftover pieces from dressmaking and salvaged good portions of work clothes to combine with muslin or purchased material. The result was quilts of infinite variety. Wheel of Fortune, Rising Sun, Broken Stone, Courthouse Square, Double T, and various string-quilt designs* were included in her repertoire.

Courthouse Square, *a quilt made by Elizabeth Borders Miller, c. 1900, for the hope chest of her daughter, Vinnye.*
(Photograph by T. Fred Miller)

Narrow strips and scraps of fabric are seamed onto a cut-paper shape such as a square or triangle and the overhanging edges of cloth trimmed. After the units are joined to make a block the paper is removed.

In addition to the utility quilts, each daughter helped make a special quilt for her wedding in a more elaborate pattern. It might be a pieced Lily or Wild Goose Chase made with all new material and an extra measure of fancy quilting. It would become the quilt reserved for guests or special occasions. The quilts carried to new homes were precious links with family and the past. They were a comfort in times of distress.

The quilting traditions in this family, as in many others, have been retained through succeeding generations. During the Great Depression quilting provided needed income for at least one of Betty's daughters, Ollie McBrayer, who quilted for other people. She also made 'on shares' a Star and Crescent quilt for her sister, receiving from her enough material to make the sister's quilt and one of her own. Other family members made quilts for themselves in the interest of economy.

The motivation for making quilts changes and yet remains the same for Betty's granddaughters, great-granddaughters, and even great-great-granddaughters in the last of the 20th century. There is still the excitement of color and design, the tactile quality of fibers, and the renewal of spirit that quiltmaking offers its practitioners.

In the 1880s most of the quilting in the South was done within the family unit. Because of the demands of rural life and the distance between residences, a day out was a rare occasion. A young Tennessee girl, Emily Murrell, described such an event while visiting relatives in Oklahoma in 1850. Her aunt was the niece of John Ross, Chief of the Cherokee Nation in Oklahoma after the removal from Tennessee in 1838.

"Monday, May 20. For the first time I saw a 'pink peony' [a flower new to Emily, at Chief John Ross's house, Rose Hill, near Tahlequah, Oklahoma]. It was indeed very beautiful. We went from Mrs. Ross's to Mrs. Vann's where we spent the day. I helped her quilt." A few days later she wrote: "As I cannot go to Min's [Min Vann's] according to promise to *help out* with quilt, I sent Margaret [a Negro] as a substitute. As Aunt Nerv is still quite unwell."

Other diaries mention neighbors or relatives who came for an interval of quilting from time to time. In much of the South, the all-day quilting bee in the 19th century was a special event occurring only occasionally with or without an accompanying corn-husking or barn-raising. Bees may have been more frequent in other locations, and literary accounts may give a somewhat romanticized view of such gatherings.

Star and Crescent *made of all new material by Ollie Miller McBrayer, Ringgold, Catoosa County, Georgia, c. 1940, for her sister, Vinnye Miller Carroll.*

(Courtesy of the Hunter Museum of Art, Chattanooga, Tennessee)

Untitled quilt. Charles Counts departs from tradition
by using designs based on organic shapes from nature,
quilted by the Rising Fawn Quilters, c. 1974.
(Photograph by T. Fred Miller)

By the end of the century more and more people were living in towns and cities and having wider social contact. New experiences and employment opportunities were changing their lives. Where an occasional quilting bee had been the highlight of the year in the past, church groups and other affiliations offered more frequent gatherings. Quilting bees for missionary societies and other worthy causes became weekly events. It was more acceptable for women to meet outside the home and assume roles of leadership. With more free time, they were able to give energy to organizing and making fund-raising quilts and endorse social and political causes.

County and state fairs, as in other parts of the country, encouraged women to show their quilts and needlework as well as products of cooking and gardening in annual competitions. Ribbons and cash awards, though small, were eagerly sought by the participants.

For 150 years or so, these county and state fairs have been organized to display agricultural and domestic skills of men, women, and children. The Flower Hall was the most popular with the women because it housed not only the beautiful garden specimens, but frequently the handwork and quilt exhibits. Viewers noted the patterns, the styles, the newest fabrics, any unusual techniques, and modeled their own work after the most impressive pieces. There was often a hasty sketch drawn or a request for a pattern from the maker of an unusual quilt. Plans were made well in advance for next year's entry. Undoubtedly the fairs played a powerful role in shaping the history of quiltmaking.

Penny McMorris, in her book *Crazy Quilts*, is of the opinion that the origin of the crazy-quilt fad occurred during the popularization of Japanese art following the Centennial Exposition in Philadelphia in 1876. The design influence may even have begun in London in 1862 with a display of Japanese art at the International Exhibition. Asymmetrical design became the mode in interior decoration, fine arts, and fancywork.

Crazy-quilt popularity swept the South, just as it did elsewhere, and many fine examples remain from this period. Basically there are three types of crazy quilts: first, the elaborate silk, velvet, and brocade quilt embellished with an impressive array of embroidery stitches; second, the wool crazy quilt also worked with stitching, perhaps a little less refined, and sometimes in wool thread; and last, the cotton-scrap crazy quilt which generally appears as a poor relative of the other two.

As with any type of quilt, there were varying degrees of proficiency and beauty. The silk quilt more often was intended as a vehicle to display the richness of one's textile collection and the prowess of the embroiderer. The colors might be vivid and strong, or deep and rich, in silk. In wool, the colors were softer, more muted and subtle, and the quilt had more practical value than a silk couch throw or table cover. As one would expect, the silks were likely to be found in metropolitan areas and many of the wools in less populated places. The cotton crazy quilt is more of a rarity and not easily categorized. Most often it seems to have been intended as a utility quilt.

As the 19th century ended, the country was growing and prospering. Advances in transportation and communication joined all regions of the country. Homemakers had the advantage of numerous gadgets to lighten work, and periodicals kept them informed of changing styles. Needlewomen were able to order patterns, fabric, and supplies by mail, giving them even more opportunities for creativity and self-expression.

The difference in domestic practices in the South and other parts of the country was primarily a matter of economics. Manufacture developed more slowly in the South than elsewhere. The agrarian society continued to predominate even though still impoverished from the effects of the Civil War. Those habits of improvisation to maintain self-sufficiency acquired during the 19th century were not easily abandoned. Daily and seasonal rituals with rural life continued to be observed long after they had disappeared in the North.

The ideal of providing and protecting one's own and the less fortunate was a basic tenet for many southern women. The responsibility for a single family was considerably less than that of a plantation mistress who had had to feed, clothe, and nurture a whole community, yet the tasks were similar. The inevitable change of seasons called for appropriate preparation. Winter following fall brought a need for warmer clothing and more bedding, and quilts were made in anticipation of their need.

In a recent year when visitors to a farm house in North Alabama were shown the upstairs beds piled high with quilts numbering, perhaps, 75, they asked their hostess the reason she had so many. "Why, we've just always made quilts in the winter. It's been our way. A body has to have something to do."

This is not an isolated instance but one that has been repeated many times in the South. The quiltmaking craft was passed down in families and communities through generations, even though fads and fashions came and went. As part of the custom, patterns were exchanged among friends and sent in letters to distant places. It was exciting when printed patterns in newspapers, farm journals, and batting wrappers began to appear. Patterns could be ordered by mail for as little as 10 cents, three for 25 cents, and quiltmakers increased their range of designs with enthusiasm. It was a challenge to try as many new patterns as time and money would allow.

A "modern" city woman who was inspired to decorate her home in the newest colonial style of the 1920s and 1930s could order a pattern by Anne Orr, Marie Webster, or Ruby McKim and make a beautiful pastel applique quilt to highlight the bedroom. Other handmade items—rugs, curtains, pillows, dresser scarves—were prepared to complement the quilt. Needlework editors described exactly how the room should look when they wrote their popular magazine columns. Improved economic conditions meant that women were more likely to be able to use all-new material, rather than scraps, in their quilts, and thus be in the latest style.

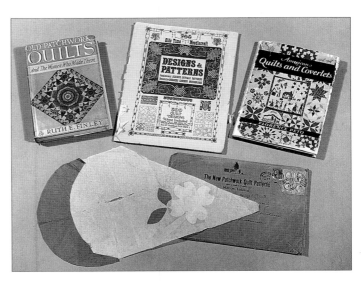

Early 20th-century books and patterns available to quiltmakers; Marie Webster's tissue Dogwood *pattern in foreground.*
(Photograph by T. Fred Miller)

Recovery came slowly, aided by the establishment of the Tennessee Valley Authority which brought electrical power to many areas of the South and encouraged new industry. By 1940 and the advent of World War II a major shift in occupations had increased the urban population. The old agrarian South had changed dramatically and, as advantages attracted rural residents to the cities, the farm way of life was left behind.

Many blacks, a generation or two removed from slavery, found city employment opportunities preferable to the uncertainties and stress of country living. While men took jobs in mills and foundries, women's work was almost entirely limited to that of domestic service or laundries. Coming from a rural environment and with limited social contact, the chance to participate in church, community, and social organizations had a profound effect upon the women and their families. They gained new educational opportunities, were exposed to change of styles and fashion, and were able to raise their standards of living.

Three women, Hattie Byrant from Commerce, Georgia, Mattie Porter of Huntsville, Alabama, and Vacie Thomas of Selmer, Tennessee, are typical of the individuals whose patterns of living changed from a rural to an urban setting when jobs beckoned black men to the city.

Hattie Bryant grew up in central Georgia on an extensive cotton plantation belonging to her parents, James and Matilda Wood. Her father was a prosperous planter who employed several hired hands in the production of cotton, the money crop. Her mother was reared in the home of James Ward of an influential white family, so that she might be educated with his children.

After they were married and had a family, Matilda became a nurse, then a lawyer, and eventually a business entrepreneur who ran a laundry during the Depression so that women might have employment. In addition to her careers, Matilda was a gifted quiltmaker who could reproduce patterns or make her own designs with great skill.

The family prospered to such an extent that each fall, after the cotton was sold, Mr. Wood gave each of his children $100 to be spent at the cotton fair in any way they chose. In the 1920s the boll weevil had so wrecked the

Matilda Wood
(Courtesy of Hattie Wood Bryant)

production of cotton that many growers were forced to sell or abandon their farms. The Woods chose to move to an urban center where they became active in business and community affairs. Hattie continues to live in the city, retains an interest in the quiltmaking she learned from her mother, and takes an active part in her church and neighborhood, always looking out for others.

Mattie Porter's father was a nurseryman in Huntsville, Alabama. Her mother was a quiltmaker and had a group of friends who quilted for each other in their homes. They did not grow cotton to have available for their quilts, but they could obtain it from neighbors who did. In the late 1930s Mattie and her husband moved to the city where he had employment in a foundry. They established themselves in their neighborhood, lived a comfortable life, and were able to provide an education for their family. Their son is a high-ranking official in city government. In her retirement years, Mattie has resumed quiltmaking with a group of senior citizens.

Vacie Thomas grew up in a household where thrift and ingenuity were fundamental. She and her sisters knew how to reclaim sugar, flour, and fertilizer sacks, boil them with lye soap in a black washpot "out back," sometimes dye them with walnut hulls, and finally iron and prepare them for quiltmaking and other household uses. Her husband's employment in the Civilian Conservation Corps (CCC) and then TVA enabled them to move to town and city. After working in a hospital for some years, Vacie enjoyed the pleasure of quiltmaking for family and friends. It was no longer the tiresome burden that it had been when she was young.

The stories of these women exemplify some of the changes that have taken place in black households. Studies by Roland Freeman in Mississippi and Laurel Horton in South Carolina indicate that some communities have resisted "progress" and retained their own distinct identity. Maude Wahlman suggests that remnants of the African culture and design continue to be transmitted within some communities removed from the mainstream of American life. These quiltmakers do many tasks in habitual ways even while incorporating new materials into routine work. They may still prefer to make scrap quilts because they like the syncopated rhythms of a quilt that has unexpected juxtaposition of assorted fabrics, but they will use polyester batting instead of hand-picked cotton of the old days.

The Freedom Quilting Bee began in 1965 in Alabama's Black Belt, in a small community called Route One, Alberta, through the efforts of white and black civil rights workers, black quiltmakers, and sympathetic friends. Forty

miles south of Selma, the region was the home of desperate, impoverished people without hope. The quiltmakers found that together they could further their cause of freedom, earn money to lift them out of poverty, and bring pride to themselves and their families. Seeking marketing outlets and working tirelessly, they succeeded in meeting many of their goals. Their quilts were a means through which they escaped a life of despair.

Mattie Ross of Gees Bend, Alabama, quilting for the Freedom Quilting Bee in 1980.
(Gee's Bend Project, John Reese, photographer; funded for the Birmingham Public Library by the National Endowment for the Humanities)

Other communities in the South have, and have had, groups using quilts as vehicles for social and political action, such as the programs offered by senior centers, government agencies, and recreational facilities. Church groups raise money for mission work, for the needy, for new kitchens, and renovated buildings by making quilts.

Quilt groups in impoverished mountain areas supply quilts for retail shops and thus earn welcome income. Quilts have been made for victims of flood, fire, earthquake, disease, and war. At least a few of these groups have been meeting for 75 years or more. At the outset of the quilt revival in the 1970s many new quilt groups and guilds were formed. At present there is no indication of decline.

In the 1960s when Charles and Rubynelle Counts moved to Lookout Mountain in Georgia, they found they were living in a locale of still-active quiltmakers. Charles Counts is a potter with an interest in many crafts and he was attracted to the work of his neighbors. Before long he was designing and making quilt tops for these women, the Rising Fawn Quilters, to quilt. He exhibited their work with his ceramics and became known as one of the innovators of the

Lillian Beattie chats with Amanda Norris at the Senior Neighbors Center, Chattanooga, Tennessee. Mrs. Beattie has had her lively quilts exhibited in a number of American art museums.
(Photograph by Mike O'Neal)

Visitors admire the work of Mrs. A. T. Davis and Mrs. C. G. Glawers at the 1953 Southern Highland Handicraft Guild's Craftsman's Fair in Gatlinburg, Tennessee.
(Courtesy of the Southern Highland Handicraft Guild, Asheville, North Carolina)

contemporary quilt movement. Then in 1971, when Jonathan Holstein and Gail van der Hoof exhibited quilts as art works at the Whitney Museum of Art in New York, quilts began to be regarded in a new way.

Alma Lesch of Shepherdsville, Kentucky began making her first quilt, a simple nine-patch, at the age of five. It was the beginning of a lifelong involvement with textiles as an artist and teacher. Her fabric collages of special garments and their associated artifacts, stitched and embellished for wall hangings, became her trademark. She, too, began exhibiting quilts as art in the 1960s, showing *Bathsheba's Bedspread* in the *Objects: USA* exhibition of contemporary crafts from the Mr. and Mrs. Samuel C. Johnson Collection of Contemporary Crafts, a milestone in the

The Rising Fawn Quilters work on a quilt by Charles Counts, c. 1974.
(Photograph by T. Fred Miller)

history of art. Her teaching has allowed many individuals to approach fiber arts with much broader understanding.

The sense of continuity and family life has always been a strong element in southern social structure. Within the family there is a strengthening of bonds of kinship, independence, obligation to state, church, and community. There is an awareness of the landscape and a regard for nature. New styles are adopted slowly and with some hesitation. The sense of tradition still is strong.

Perhaps it cannot be claimed that quilting in the South is distinctly different from that of other places, but certain regional tendencies do seem to exist. While the methods for gathering quilt information vary from one state quilt research project to another, the results allow us to see the likenesses and differences of the quilts from each particular section of the country.

Blue Patchwork Cross, detail, made by Pamona Louvicy Forester Stuart, 1895–6, Sugar Creek, Hickman County, Tennessee. After piecing the top, she put it away in order to assist her husband in building their house. It was quilted by her daughter, Bertha May Stuart Bolton, in 1930.
(Photograph by David Luttrell, courtesy of the Quilts of Tennessee)

Feathered Star, *detail, pieced, quilted, and stuffed by Victoria Darwin Caldwell, Spring City, Rhea County, Tennessee, 1865.*

(Photograph by David Luttrell, courtesy of the Quilts of Tennessee)

Volunteers hang an antique palampore bedcover from India during a quilt documentation session in 1974. (Photograph by T. Fred Miller)

Quilt researchers in southern states found a strong preference for scrap quilts by regional quiltmakers. The difference between southern scrap quilts and those of Pennsylvania and Ohio, for example, lies in the source of the scraps. In the North, the scraps were new material of good quality left from dressmaking and other quilt projects. Their counterparts were made from anything available and might include salvaged parts of used garments, recycled sacks, and a variety of scraps more inclusive than the better cotton dress scraps. Even today there are quilters who will buy new material and mix it up to give the offbeat variety of a scrap quilt.

The researchers in these same states have recorded fine examples of chintz quilts which had such popularity along the eastern coast. Some of these quilts were taken from their original locations as their owners sought new opportunities or adventure. Fine workmanship denotes makers trained in needle arts and with leisure time, women whose lives were quite different from those who might be living in a sod house on the central plains.

The chintz applique quilts may have been the inspiration for some of the handsome applique quilts originating in North Carolina, East Tennessee, and Kentucky. Without ready access to imported fabric, a quiltmaker could cut out her own floral arrangement from available cloth and make a quilt of equal quality and refinement. Of course, applique quilts have been made in all parts of the country. Even so, a certain delicacy of line, less vivid color, and regional styles of quilting seem to set some of the southern quilts apart. There are the usual red and green fabrics, but, combined with pinks and yellows, the impression is less bold than many of the applique quilts of northern states.

Before air conditioning made summertime more bearable, consideration was given to tempering hot weather in all possible ways. High ceilings, dark window shades, cross ventilation, and wide verandas were part of the defense. Light colors reflected sunlight and, of themselves, looked less oppressive. It followed naturally that quilts made in the deep South might have more white background and lighter colors. Some quilted bedcovers were all white, without piecing or applique. The white wholecloth quilt continued to be made in the South long after its production had ceased in other places.

The findings in the Tennessee survey indicated that quilts made in middle Tennessee in the last third of the 19th century were much darker than those made in east Tennessee. This practice was attributed to the devastation and economic collapse suffered in middle Tennessee as a result of the Civil War. Many raids and bloody battles occurred there as well as ransacking of private homes by soldiers of both armies. The quilts seem to show the distress and hardships that shadowed the area for years afterward.

Dyeing with natural materials continued to be practiced in the South well into the 20th century. Some of today's quiltmakers recall, as children, gathering walnut hulls, oak and maple bark, or red clay to put into an iron pot for a dye bath. (A dyed quilt lining reduced the frequency for laundering since it was less likely to "show the soil.") Other methods of

dyeing included the complicated procedures necessary for indigo and turkey-red as well as the easy-to-use commercial packets produced for home dyeing.

It is likely that further investigation will uncover isolated patterns and practices not found in other locations. In Tennessee, Rhea County quilters continued the technique of stuffed work, on both pieced and applique quilts, as late as 1910, long after it had generally been abandoned. The pieced rose pattern of 1850-1880 has been noted in greater numbers in Tennessee than in other states. The Rocky Mountain Road pattern was seen in many color combinations, in different scales, and set on diagonal as well as in straight arrangements. The earliest and finest was made as a wedding quilt in 1840. When the same pattern appeared in South Carolina, it was usually set on the vertical-horizontal plane and construction was somewhat imperfect, as though it might have been a training piece.

It is difficult to discover the origins of 19th-century quilt patterns; but one, a rosette-like shape appliqued in block design, was found repeatedly during the North Carolina survey. It seems most likely, because of the prevalence, that the pattern originated there. Several names and interpretations have been given to the design, Plume-Circle among them. Sixteen examples were found in the Piedmont region and seem to have been made about 1850-1890. A single, similar example was found in each of the states of South Carolina, Missouri, and Tennessee, the maker of the latter having connections with North Carolina relatives. It was common practice to share patterns with friends afar and seldom did a quilt design remain so isolated as this one had.

The first domestic textile mills were established in New England and produced goods of fine quality in abundance, only to have the supply to the South cut off during the Civil War. Home weaving was reinstituted and continued until the war ended and trade resumed. Within a few years the southern textile industry began to expand and produce in impressive quantities. Much of the fabric of the last part of the 19th century was printed in one color—blue, black, gray, or dark red—on a medium to poor quality cloth and therefore was inexpensive to produce. The retail price was low enough for almost every quilter to afford, and the cloth does, indeed, appear time after time in the quilts from that period.

Styles of quilting are less well documented than patterns and fabrics. The differences are more subtle and less obvious, making comparisons more difficult. However, looking at quilts in a circumscribed region reveals the quiltmakers' preferences for patterns of quilting such as allover parallel rows used

A modern quilter works on a polyester-filled quilt which requires less quilting than one filled with cotton. (Photograph by Gail Andrews Trechsel)

alone or as background filler, either in the straight or diagonal direction; straight or diagonal crosshatched rows; allover clamshell or wineglass (overlapping circles) shapes; and the quarter-circle concentric rows called shell, elbow, Methodist, Baptist, or fan quilting. The latter is most often seen on utility quilts because of its ease of execution: it follows the natural movement of the arm. The elbow is used as a compass point in drawing an arc and repeating it across the quilt. Parallel arcs are dropped below the original mark to fill in the space.

Kathy Sullivan, who coordinated the North Carolina quilt study, has observed that 19th-century North Carolina quilting seems less sophisticated than that found in the North and lacks refinement. When comparisons are made with antique "company" quilts from Ohio, it looks as though the North Carolina quilting patterns had been repeatedly passed on to the

Crown of Thorns (Rocky Mountain *or* New York Beauty)
was made *by Mrs. D. P. Walker, Sweetwater Valley,
Monroe County, Tennessee, c. 1840 as a wedding quilt
for her daughter. The quilting is exceedingly fine.*
(Photograph by David Luttrell, courtesy of the Quilts of Tennessee)

extent that they have lost the original crispness of configurations. Perhaps it is this lack of perfection, the naive quality, which gives a certain charm to old southern quilts.

Floral quilting designs on wholecloth or in the white spaces between applique and pieced blocks appear on many southern quilts made before 1850. It is not unusual for the motif to change, to be different, in each square. Rows of background quilting were often combined with the floral designs to produce a surface of close quilting and create a motif in bas-relief. The stitching rows of this stipple quilting were sometimes as close as three-sixteenths or one-fourth of an inch. The close quilting technique continued to be used much longer in the South than it did in the North.

The character of the quilt lining is another category for comparison. Many southern quilt backs were made with handwoven material or coarsely woven mill cloth. The word *handwoven* does not necessarily imply that the thread was handspun. Southern textile mills produced sufficient quantities of thread to supply many weavers. Loom production in the home was widely practiced before the Civil War, and even in households that had ceased weaving, a revival was necessitated by the war blockade. Northern mill production supplied fine percales for its quiltmakers, but southerners were more likely to use coarser cotton checks such as Alamance plaids or plain or dyed muslin, if not their own handwoven cloth, for their quilt backs.

Quilting thread, too, was often of a somewhat coarser quality, which did not allow for refined stitches and contributed to greater surface texture. Even in the 1900s southern quilters were still using the balls of heavy thread so long a part of their home supplies. The total commitment to thrift fostered by the Depression included saving the string with which sacks were stitched. It was wound in a ball and saved for the quilting of everyday quilts.

Quilts do look alike, but when they are studied in large numbers within a given boundary, it is possible to discover ever so slight variations to set them apart. Putting all the differences together and comparing the quilts with those from other places may gradually reveal a distinct regional character. I hope that the clues provided here will enable others to distinguish more of the qualities that give the flavor of the South.

From European traditions and other cultural heritage, southern quiltmakers have developed their craft. In choosing to write about one corner of the United State we have used generalizations and a few examples to present the background that is available to today's quiltmakers. The state surveys have added immeasurable information to the knowledge of family structure and accompanying social, economic, and political influences. The vignettes of domestic life, combined with accounts of soldiers and wars, commerce and politics, will enlarge and enrich our rendering of southern history.

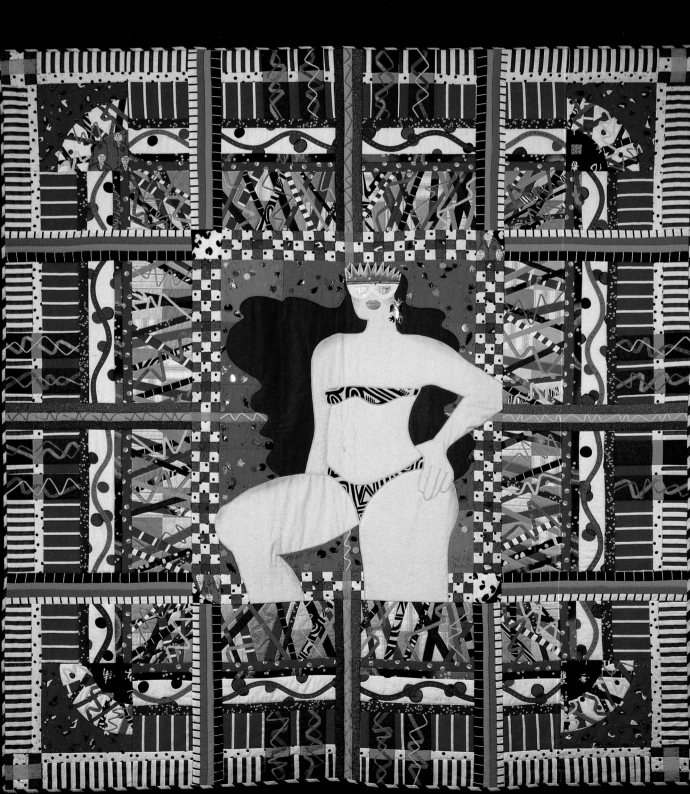

The Departures
by
Gail Andrews Trechsel

Of the many forms of artistic expression in America, the handmade quilt is the most beloved and, perhaps therefore, the most traditional. For generations a symbol of home and hearth, industry and thrift, comfort and security, the American quilt changed little. Now that contemporary fiber artists are making quilts, however, old ways are giving way to new—to new materials, unconventional colors and designs, even changes in forms. Such innovations excite viewers but also challenge preconceptions of many people, leaving them startled and confused.

To better understand the work of contemporary artists using quilts and fabrics as their media, it helps to look at developments in art in the 20th century. The Arts and Crafts Movement, a reaction to the Industrial Revolution in England, affected American artists and design as well. Extending from 1875 to 1920, the movement was led by social reformers who lamented not only the lack of good design and craftsmanship in machine-made objects, but the fact that machines and division of labor were depriving the craftsman of the pleasure of his work.

The Movement's great concern for the worker found its political expression in Socialism that paralleled the spreading anti-aristocratic political sentiments. It was no accident that designs came to be valued for their simplicity, lack of pretension, and evidence of connection with their maker. Artists often purposely left hammer or chisel marks on their objects as evidence that the pieces were crafted by hand. There was also an attempt to revive handicraft skills of the Middle Ages. In the field of textiles, ancient dye formulas were reinstituted, as well as the delicate embroidery styles of the 14th and 15th centuries.

A major principle of the Arts and Crafts Movement was the belief that the objects with which a person lived had a direct influence on his character. Handmade articles that expressed ideals of honesty and sincerity, it was believed, would produce individuals with those same qualities.

The most visible proponent of the Arts and Crafts Movement was the English writer/ designer/craftsman William Morris. Morris was among the first to dismiss the notion of a division between fine art and crafts. As Jonathan Fairbanks states in *The Eloquent Object*, Morris believed that a "contemplative worker who produced excellently crafted work was also an artist."

The Movement in America was promoted by Gustav Stickley and his magazine, *The Craftsman*, published from 1901 to 1916. As the philosophy gained recognition in America, enthusiasm for the handmade object grew. Interiors were simplified and painters and sculptors began working in areas previously associated with crafts (furniture, pottery, textiles), designing useful objects in response to the poorly made and unattractive machine-made counterparts.

Another important aspect of the Arts and Crafts Movement was the involvement of women as professional artists working in clay, wood, silver, glass, and other media. Until the last quarter of the 19th century, the opportunities for women to receive training in the visual arts had been limited, especially in the American South. Now it became easier for them to train with skilled artists and pursue careers (beyond teaching) in the visual arts.

Concurrent with the Arts and Crafts Movement in America came a revived interest and enthusiasm for American decorative arts of the 18th and 19th centuries. Many collectors and museums began to value American decorative arts and consider them worthy of study. The interest in early American furniture, textiles, and other objects did not always spring from an interest in hand crafts, however. It came also from an interest in history and antiques, an appreciation that often inhibited originality and fostered imitation.

This Colonial Revival period, together with the outbreak of World War I, shifted attention away from many of the principles of the Arts and Crafts Movement, stifling creativity. Indeed, the fascination with reproductions affected all media. Penny McMorris and Michael Kile describe its impact on quiltmaking in *The Art Quilt*: "The Colonial Revival moved quiltmaking away from originality and toward mere replication. . . . This rote copying violated the very spirit of the earlier Arts and Crafts movement—and of quiltmaking."

Closer to the philosophy of the Arts and Crafts Movement than the Colonial Revival was the revival of handicrafts in the Appalachian Mountains of the South, documented by Allen Eaton's study, *Handicrafts of the Southern Highlands*. Eaton describes various traditional crafts of the region and offers brief histories of the schools, handicraft centers, and home projects established to preserve handicrafts and train new generations in skill and appreciation.

Many schools and centers were established in Appalachia during the first quarter of the 20th century. Among the most influential were Berea College, with its Fireside Industries, in Kentucky; the Pi Beta Phi Settlement School (now Arrowmont) in Tennessee; Penland Weavers and Potters, the John C. Campbell Folk School, and the Allanstand Cottage Industries, all in North Carolina. Their objective was to preserve and revive native handicrafts, develop markets for the goods, and boost the incomes and self-respect of the makers.

In December, 1929 a group of individuals representing these centers gathered in Asheville, North Carolina, and organized the Southern Highland Handicraft Guild. Allen Eaton and Olive Dame Campbell (Mrs. John C. Campbell) took the lead in forming this organization. The Guild is very active today with more than 700 individual members plus 100 active centers representing another 1,500 individuals. It continues to encourage the best in craftsmanship and individuality of expression and endeavors to expand the market for the works of artists in the region through sales, promotion and special exhibitions.

Although there are statewide guilds around the country, the Southern Highland Guild is unusual in representing artists over such a broad geographic area; members are drawn from the nine states of the Appalachians. Marian Heard, a founder of Arrowmont and its director from 1946–1977, has been involved with the Guild for most of its existence. She notes that the Guild was very early in recognizing the need for this type of support organization and says it is unique in the mix of traditional and contemporary member artists. There are now second-and-third generation artists in the Guild. This may be a testament to the benefits of membership, or to the peristence of tradition in the South.

All of the teachers and administrators of the programs established in the early decades of this century believed in the beauty of handwork and the dignity of the craftsman. Recalling the doctrines of the Arts and Crafts Movement, Allen Eaton described the joy the craftsman finds not only in the creation of his work, but in his materials as well; and how the wood, the wool, and the clay bring him close to nature, and thus to the source of all art.

The development of these various movements in the southern mountains was followed by the Great Depression and several government-established agencies, including the Works Progress Administration (WPA) Federal Arts Project. Social concerns in America reached an all-

NIGHT THOUGHTS II
Susan Wilchins
Cotton broadcloth, heavy cotton twill backing, synthetic
    lamé hand dyeing, screen printing; machine piecing,
    machine applique, machine quilting
57"x 57", 1990
Collection of the artist

LEAF SYMMETRY III
Nancy Whittington
Silk, some fabric hand dyed and painted; machine
  piecing, English template piecing, hand applique,
  hand quilting
49½″ x 48″, 1989
Collection of the artist
Photograph by Doug Van de Zande

time high. The purpose of the WPA's arts project was to give employment to artists, craftsmen, and photographers. According to Rose Slivka, writing in *The Eloquent Object*, the WPA gave commissions to "up to 5,300 artists and craftsmakers annually during its eight-year span, not only providing a living for many developing artists but also validating art as worthwhile work in the American social structure."

Less has been written about the WPA handicrafts projects than the programs supporting fine arts, although it is known that approximately 3,000 different handicraft projects were supported across the country. One distinction between the two was made by Andy Harney, who noted that most of the individuals employed for the fine arts projects were skilled artists. On the other hand, in most handicrafts projects, trained artists and craftsmen were assigned to supervise unskilled workers. These projects often were set up to provide income to individuals, especially women, who did not fit easily into other work-relief programs. Weaving and quilting were among the crafts taught.

The studio craftsman who emerged from the WPA days is the inheritor of the rich tradition of the handicrafts movement begun at the turn of the century in America. As early as 1900 instruction in the crafts had begun appearing in some American universities. Among the most important teaching centers was Black Mountain College, which was nestled in the foothills of the Blue Ridge Mountains overlooking the town of Black Mountain, North Carolina (1933–1956). Though Black Mountain was a communal, liberal arts college, the studio arts were its central discipline. In the words of its founder, John Andrew Rice, art was to be "at the very center of things."

Several artists associated with the Bauhaus School in Germany taught at Black Mountain, most notably, Josef Albers. The aim of the Bauhaus, in the words of its director Walter Gropius, was "the unification of all training in art and design. . . . in which no barriers exist between the structural and decorative arts." Students studying fine arts could become proficient in various craft processes, and the trained artist could also use the machine to advantage. Philosophically, the artist had a responsibility to society which could be reflected in quality design for mass production of objects for daily use.

Other important schools were founded in the 30s, the most prominent of which was the Cranbrook Academy of Art, officially begun in 1932, in Michigan. In the South, early centers (besides Black Mountain) include Peabody College in Nashville and the crafts program established at the University of Tennessee in 1936 by Marian Heard. Such centers gave Americans the opportunity to study with some of Europe's best craftsmen and designers and offered exposure and training in the ideals of various European interpretations of the Arts and Crafts Movement, the Bauhaus and later the International Style. The European artists, the majority from Germany, Austria, and Scandinavia, had a profound influence on American design and art education. Although Cranbrook, in particular, had as a goal training artists to produce objects of quality for daily life, all the institutions continued to advocate the value of handwork per se. Their greatest impact, especially at Black Mountain, was on art education.

Josef Albers, newly arrived from Germany, taught at Black Mountain from its inception until 1949. He saw art as applicable to every facet of life and his teaching reflected the Bauhaus method of learning about different materials and techniques through actual application. As Albers wrote, "art is not an object but experience." This method opened the door for artists to experiment with, and combine, media, leading various disciplines to become less insular.

The new teaching methods contributed to the rise of Abstract Expressionism in America, stressing individualism and the artist's interaction with his materials. Artists, primarily painters, became actively involved with the process of making art, more concerned with the process of applying paint than with questions of content. Their expression was driven by interior, psychic forces; and many of the artists were influenced by Existentialism, the philosophy that stresses the uniqueness of individual experience and freedom of choice in life. Students of crafts, to no one's surprise, became active participants in Abstract Expressionism along with painters and sculptors.

The end of World War II brought a tremendous expansion of craft instruction in American universities. Many veterans, continuing their educations under the GI Bill, chose crafts as their major field. This expansion of craft instruction spurred greater diversity in the subjects taught. The growth in university departments and curricula continued through the 60s, providing employment for many of the craftsmen trained in the system. According to Edward Lucie-Smith, building skills and technical knowledge was what was important. "The production of work to be sold in the marketplace was not the primary goal."

By the 1960s employment opportunities for craftspeople within universities were dimimishing, and many artists left the university system. The 60s also brought revolt against the existing political and social structures. Many individuals rebelled against "the system" by dropping out of it and going to live in rural areas. These new living situations were sometimes communal, sometimes individual. Many of the people searching for alternative lifestyles were artists and craftsmen who attempted to support themselves by the sale of their work.

The public mood was ripe for a return to objects that showed evidence of their maker. The renewed enthusiasm for the handmade object was similar to the reaction against industrialization in the 19th century. Consumers were tired of machine-produced standardization and celebrated the beauty of the individually made and created object. Their appreciation began to show in commerical markets. During the 1970s and 1980s the art market boomed, generating more galleries specializing in ceramics, glass, metals, and fiber.

Although artists working in fiber comprise the largest numbers, fiber ironically is often treated as a stepchild in exhibitions, publications, and sales. Many reasons have been variously expressed. It is sometimes argued that fiberworks are difficult to show and install. There is a fear of the sometimes fugitive nature of the materials and dyes that could make them unstable for long-term installations. Usually unstated, and perhaps unrealized but internalized, is a prejudice that fiber, long associated with women and women's work, is not as prestigious as other materials.

In the 1960s another movement—the women's movement—began calling attention to inequities in opportunities offered women artists. Their demands helped to change university curricula, hiring practices, legislation, and art itself. In 1971, artists Judy Chicago and Miriam Schapiro founded the Feminist Art Program at the California Institute of Arts in Valencia. Both artists promote making art of women's experiences. Chicago, famous for her feminist work, "The Dinner Party," uses female images in her pieces; Schapiro's imagery is more subtle but no less strident.

Schapiro began to incorporate fabric into her paintings in the 1970s. She used remnants of feminine handwork such as lace, embroidery, and quilts. Demanding the viewer to reconsider these objects and their makers, the

TENNESSEE WALTZ
Elizabeth Cherry Owen
Cotton, cotton velvet, silk and wool blends, poly-cotton,
    hand painted fabrics, indigo dyed shibori, dyes and
    acrylic fabric paints, photograms; machine piecing,
    hand reverse applique, hand quilting
63″x 68″, 1990
Collection of the artist

VOLCANIC ACTIVITY
Ellen Kochansky
Textile collage of various fabrics; embroidery, painting,
    machine quilting
72″x 48″, 1990
Collection of the artist

artist called her assemblages femmages. "I choose to use fabric in the decorative arts," she explained, "as tangible symbols for my connection to domesticity and to express my belief that art resides in domesticity. For me, the fabric of my art and the fabric of my life neatly equate each other."

Schapiro's enthusiasm for quilts and other needlework paralleled the second 20th-century quilt revival in America (the first was in the 1930s). Thanks to the tremendous craft revival in the 1960s Americans were inspired not only to buy pottery, quilts, jewelry, and other decorative and functional art objects, they began trying their own hands at making some of these things. An explosion of classes, workshops, books, and exhibitions erupted, especially in quiltmaking.

One of the first exhibitions, and certainly the pivotal exhibition in stimulating contemporary appreciation for antique quilts, was held at the Whitney Museum in New York in 1971. Two collectors, Jonathan Holstein and Gail van der Hoof, approached the Whitney with the idea of exhibiting 19th-century pieced quilts, not as historical artifacts, but as works of art chosen on the basis of how they worked as paintings. The exhibition was entitled "Abstract Design in American Quilts." Quilts were hung on gallery walls as if they were large, abstract paintings. The effect was monumental and far-reaching and the quilts met critical acclaim. Hilton Kramer writing in *The New York Times* stated that "the anonymous quiltmakers of the American provinces created a remarkable succession of visual masterpices." The critic at *The New Yorker* magazine wrote, "A quilt that looks merely homey lying at the foot of a bed may become a great work of abstract design when it is hung on an enormous white wall."

The Whitney exhibition toured in America and abroad. Soon, quilts began appearing in other exhibitions, galleries, and auction sales. These antique quilts were appreciated for their aesthetics. People marveled at the sophisticated patterns and dramatic combinations of color, and the quilts were compared to large, contemporary paintings.

Historians working to shed light on groups of Americans ignored by previous histories embraced quilts as links with women of the 19th century. When it was discovered that not all of the exhibited quilts were by "anonymous women," serious scholarship began in quilt history. Feminists recognized quilts as a creative medium employed by individuals denied alternative forms of self-expression.

Artists in other media, not necessarily active in the women's movement, began experimenting with the possibilities and challenges offered by fabric. Some artists created quilts based upon traditional models. Their quilts were hung on the wall, but they still were functional bedcovers. They displayed bold graphic designs and startling juxtapositions of color; but they were, for the most part, constructed from cotton fabrics in traditional techniques of piecing and applique. Variation in design and color was valued, but most quilts were built around the long-standard repeating grid format. Other artists, trained in a variety of disciplines, were

fascinated and moved by the beauty of the quilt and its tactile nature; but they felt hemmed in by the boundaries imposed by the prevailing perception of what a quilt was supposed to look like.

The realization by artists that they could use a passion for fabric in their work inevitably brought a new form to the quilt. Many of the quilt artists working today were trained as painters, printmakers or weavers, but are self-taught as quilters. They are using their formal knowledge of art plus their enthusiasm and curiosity for the special qualities of fabric to explore issues of color, texture, pattern, and surface elaboration.

The 28 artists selected for *Southern Quilts: A New View*, include individuals who studied art and worked as potters, printmakers, jewelers, but also includes a social worker, a biochemist and the former principal flutist with the Arkansas Symphony. Their materials include cloth but also acetate, Mylar, animal hides, socks and plastic flowers. They remain uninhibited by convention and are open to the techniques and materials of the world around them. The only stipulation made by the curators of this exhibition was that the pieces must possess a top, middle, and back and be fastened together in some way. Some pieces undoubtedly will evoke negative reactions. "But that's not a quilt!" The best of any art challenges the perceptions of its audience. Quilts, icons in American life, possess audiences that understandably cling to somewhat rigid conceptions of what a quilt should be. They may come to enjoy some of the new quilts, however, by realizing that studio quilt artists are not trying to replace, or even compete with, the makers of traditional quilts. They are merely expressing themselves in a medium that offers opportunities other mediums do not.

The concept of the studio quilt artist did not exist 20 years ago. By the mid-70s exhibitions began focusing on the art quilt or studio quilt, notably "The New American Quilt" at the Museum of Contemporary Crafts in New York and, most influential, the biennial juried exhibitions sponsored by the Southeastern Ohio Cultural Arts Center known as "Quilt National," which hosted its first exhibition in 1979.

In the South, a few museums, universities, and commercial galleries have broadened the audience of contemporary quilters. The Southern Quilt Symposium sponsored by the Hunter Museum in Chattanooga with its 1986 exhibition, "New Quilts of the Mid-South," is but one example of this trend among museums. The Signature Shop in Atlanta was one of the first galleries in the South providing a showcase for fiber arts.

What studio quilters across the country have in common is their relish for the flexibility of fabric. In the words of quilt artist and author, Michael James, (One) "can deal with problems of design with a directness that other forms do not offer. Color is not merely *on* the surface; it is *in* the fiber. Shape is not merely outlined; its contours—the edges of the fabric pieces—can be felt and manipulated in a way that no drawn or painted shape can be. Figures . . . . can be experienced both front and back . . . . and generally manipulated in ways that they could not were they purely two dimensional."

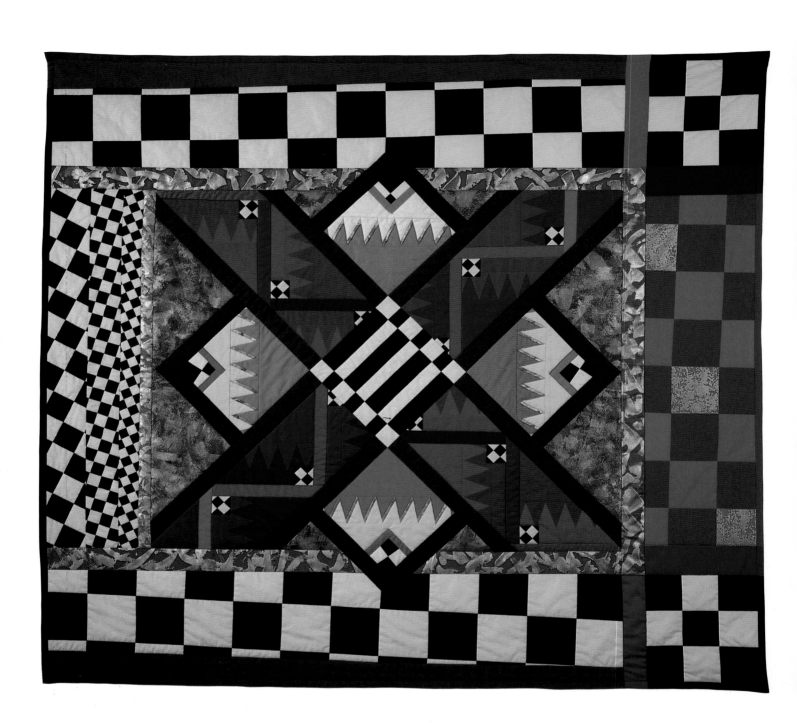

THRESHOLD III
Patsy Allen
Cotton, fabric paint; machine piecing, applique, quilting
58"x 52", 1990
Collection of the artist

THE SMALL CITY
Lenore Davis
Cotton sateen, monotype printing and painting with
   fiber reactive dyes, textile paints; tacking, cotton
   backing
70"x 70", 1990
Collection of the artist

The Artists

SUSAN WILCHINS

One of the exhibition artists whose work extracts the ultimate in fabric's potential is Susan Wilchins. Her lush expressions dazzle the viewer with their complexity of pattern and richness of color and texture. She chooses fabrics specifically "for their ability to communicate tactile and textural ideas." In "Night Thoughts II" (page 44), one in a series of her works exploring the Earth, she uses many dense, rich layers of fabric to suggest the layers of moss, lichens, leaves, and sticks one might find on a forest floor.

The overall pattern achieved through the layering is beautiful, but one must look further into the piece to discover the details that give the overall design its power. Just as nature draws us to study the lichen on a log, this quilt top draws us to the smaller elements that form the composition.

Wilchins combines traditional quilting techniques of piecing, applique, and embroidery with contemporary techniques of screen printing and controlled dyeing. She screen-prints white cotton fabric in a variety of colors and images (the images come from her photographs of leaves and tree limbs). She then tears the printed fabric into strips about an inch wide. These strips are rearranged and sewn with other strips (the seams on the surface of the fabric) to create new lengths of cloth. These strips are then cut again and re-sewn. This new cloth with its patchwork of color and texture form the backgrounds of her quilts.

The pieces are cut, rearranged, and sewn to a heavy backing and then the entire piece is washed and dried to encourage fraying of the fabric edges. Finally, other pieces are cut and applied over the surface to complete the composition. Untrimmed threads add to the multiplicity of layers.

"Night Thoughts II" is complex and full of energy. But it is not a frenetic energy. To meander through "Night Thoughts" is a peaceful experience. Among the fabrics is a pale blue-green lamé, a color and material that punctuates the design and offers spots of repose.

POODLE QUILT
Susan Webb Lee
Cotton; machine piecing, strip piecing, machine quilting
58"x 54", 1989
Collection of the artist

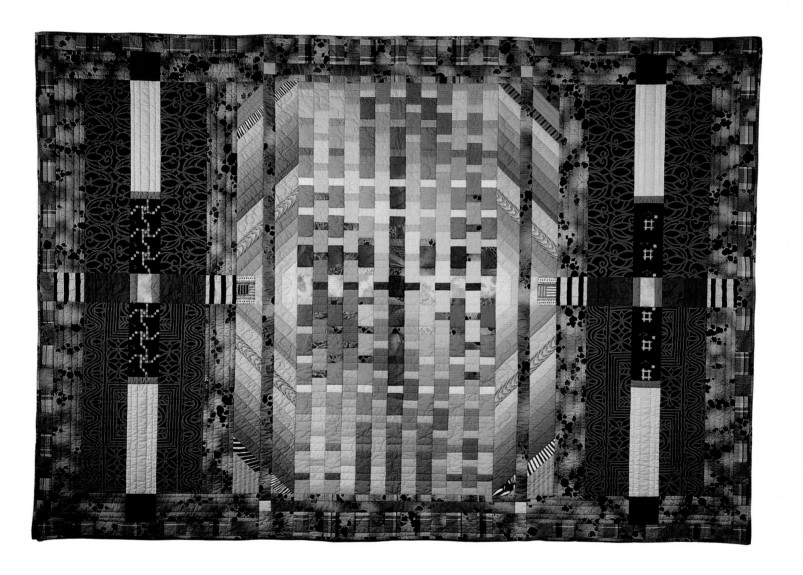

BARRIER GATE
Mary Jo Dalrymple
Hand dyed, overdyed, tie dyed cotton, American fabrics
   with the exception of ikat from Japan and
   silkscreened cotton from Kenya; machine piecing,
   hand quilting
68"x 94", 1988
Collection of the artist

NANCY WHITTINGTON

Another artist mesmerized by the natural world around her is Nancy Whittington. In "Leaf Symmetry III," (page 45) Whittington continues work on a series of quilts which are based on an interlocking leaf shape and square pattern. Fascinated by color and light, she says that all of the quilts in this series "portray a quality of radiance, a surface touched by light."

The fabric chosen for her quilt is silk, many pieces hand-dyed and painted. Its lustrous surface is particularly well suited to the composition and the interplay of color.

The colors of the quilt range from grays to pinks to yellows in subtle and harmonious gradations, yielding the inner glow that the artist envisioned. The fragile nature of the silk relates to the fragility of our natural world. The silk, very susceptible to the pulls and punctures of the sewing machine, reminds us of the ephemeral quality of all life.

ELIZABETH CHERRY OWEN

The exploration of color and color relationships figures prominently in the work of most of these artists. Elizabeth Cherry Owen uses an extensive range of fabric painting and surface design techniques to achieve her emotionally-charged compositions. The colors employed in "Tennessee Waltz" (page 48) are brilliant and gay, but they cannot disguise, nor are they meant to, the desperation and tension one feels when viewing this work as a whole.

"Tennessee Waltz" expresses the artist's attempt to bring understanding and order to a turbulent year in her life and is "an unusually direct expression of personal loss." The artist continues, "This piece serves as a reminder to me and to the viewer of the artificiality of the structure which we seek to impose on our lives. The result of this attempt is a sort of ordered chaos, depicted by the quadrilateral forms which compose the piece, often interrupted by events over which we have no control. I used color to create a feeling of ambiguous, shifting space and to express the emotions I felt during this period of my life."

Large, amoeba-like shapes float over the surface grid of the quilt symbolizing the artist's loss. The shapes become holes reminding us of the emptiness loss brings. Owen writes that the smaller shapes represent the ripples of these events, which continue to interrupt the structure of her life. The quilting emphasizes these biomorphic shapes.

Owen says that Jasper Johns' series of "Crosshatch" paintings from the 1970s and 1980s, particulary the random structure of the paintings, were a source of inspiration for this piece. Her interest in modern painting and formal concerns of color and structure show in her work. Her pieces are painterly, but she feels very strongly attached to fabric and traditional techniques of piecing, applique, and quilting.

ELLEN KOCHANSKY

Ellen Kochansky, another artist who takes a painterly approach to quiltmaking, draws on her background in costume design and theatre and her love of color and fabric. Kochansky states that paint and the blankness of the canvas were alien to her, and that her involvement with costume and fashion design generated a passion for cloth and "all the visual, sensual, and sentimental imagery associated with quilts."

In "Volcanic Activity," (page 49) as in many of her works, the artist creates panels of fabric of rich, textural color using techniques that include overdyeing, layering, transparent fabrics, and coloring with airbrushed dyes and pigments. The panels are machine embroidered with several kinds of thread, then slit into strips and reconstructed. She uses the order imposed by the vertical strips as a foil, emphasizing what she calls the chaos of the fabric surface. Mauves, blues and yellows shimmer into the starkness of the white and gray fabric strips and create a moody and atmospheric composition. The piece shows Kochansky's obvious love for cloth and her "gluttony for color."

MIDNIGHT CONVERSATIONS
Murray Johnston
Cotton, poly-cotton; machine piecing, hand applique,
 hand quilting
60″x 50″, 1990
Collection of the artist

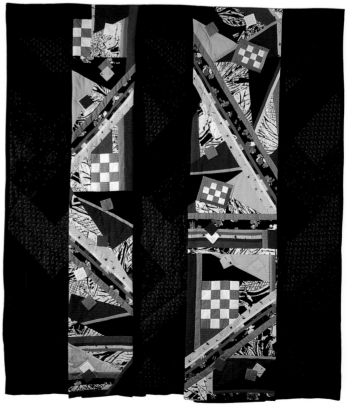

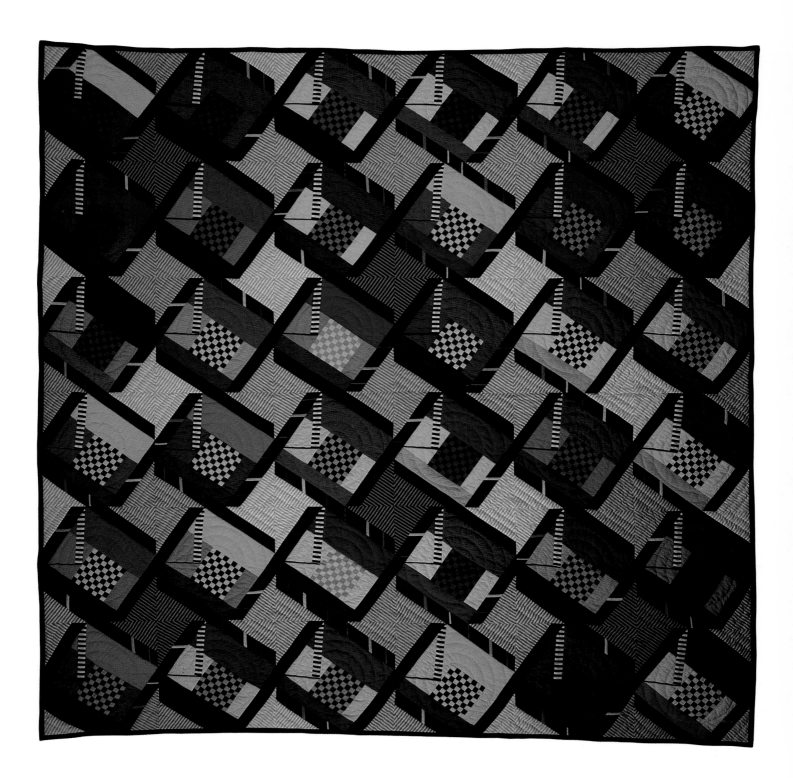

THE FAT LADY SINGS
Sharon Heidingsfelder
Cotton, silkscreened; machine piecing, hand quilting
70"x 70", 1987
Collection of the artist

PATSY ALLEN

In spite of love for the medium, some artists feel the expression is more important than the materials. One is Patsy Allen, whose work has evolved from weaving to fabric constructions to quilts. She states that her medium has changed before, so it could change again. The exploration and expression of her idea is what is important. "Like many others, I came to quiltmaking with an art background. The issues that I deal with are the same formal ones of interest to many artists: color, light, space, and pattern."

In much of Allen's work we see sharp, crisp colors clearly defining a space or repeating a pattern. Art Deco motifs have been important influences in her quilts. In her more recent work, Allen plays with the illusion of space and how we perceive it.

She points out that in "Threshold III" (page 52) "a new sense of space is becoming evident. I say becoming because many ideas are revealed to me only after I'm well into a series. The Threshold Series uses bold architectural elements and a defined space that is at the same time ambiguous. One may ask, 'Are these shapes coming out to meet me or am I going in to greet them?' The threshold entreats one to enter and at the same time to pause."

A new element in this work is the inclusion of hand-painted fabrics and the black and white fabric that borders the quilt. Gold pigment plays against a blue ground on the hand-painted fabric, giving the material a sheen, a richness and preciousness. Black and white squares at the base of the quilt recede as one approaches the painted surface, propelling the viewer into this special space.

Folded triangles of cloth, similar to pressed piecing, add a dimension to the surface impossible to achieve with a painted surface alone. The narrowing strips of fabric on the vertical borders lead our eye up, adding to the verticality of the piece, focusing our view on the large central square which emphasizes the threshold aspect.

LENORE DAVIS

One cannot help feeling the architectural quality of "The Small City" (page 53) by Lenore Davis. The artist printed and painted a series of patterns on a solid ground, building a whole patterned cloth in much the same way as squares of fabric are sewn together. The finished composition resembles a large tile wall.

Davis received her initial training in ceramics and spent a year furthering this study in Portugal. Since 1969 she has worked in fabric and has used various surface painting and dyeing techniques. In "The Small City" her love of paint, quilts, printmaking, and ceramic tiles merge in a delightful composition.

"The Small City" has a strong graphic quality and is equally exciting when viewed from a distance or studied at close range. Davis points out that the major excitement in the work comes from the repetition of the print. She uses small images, but when they are compounded the whole becomes very dynamic.

Much of Davis's previous work involves the human figure expressed in soft sculpture. She uses pigment on both her three-dimensional figures and her wall pieces, and color is an important aspect of her work. Whimsey is also an important element in many of Davis's pieces and it plays a role in "The Small City" as well. The boldly-painted border appears to be a spoof of the familiar feathered-wreath and feathered-star motifs and adds a fanciful quality to the quilt.

SUE ALVAREZ

Some of the best contemporary work celebrates traditional quilt forms with a dynamic twist. Sue Alvarez frequently uses the basic nine patch in her work—but watch out! Under her needle, traditional patterns explode with color and often humor.

In "Beach Games" (page 40) the central square of the quilt is dominated by a female figure clad in the skimpiest of bikinis. What draws our attention, however, is not the brevity of the swimwear, but the size of the wearer. The woman has thighs like tree trunks. As she coolly stares at us, we applaud her brazenness. Alvarez says the sunglasses, a gift from her husband, inspired this particular bathing beauty.

The quilt is enlivened by exuberant fabrics, ribbons and sequins, which compose and adorn the surface. Narrow ribbons snake over polka dots and stripes, spangles catch and reflect the light, and bold colors vie for our attention. In spite of what might seem to be wild, however, there is an underlying order and stability given to the piece by its strict geometric construction.

Several artists included in this survey cite quiltmaker Nancy Crow as a source of their inspiration. Sue Alvarez also studied with Crow and admires Crow's work and drive. "I never had anyone look at my work and say, 'that's good, now what?' " Alvarez says Crow taught her not to be easily satisfied and always to push herself.

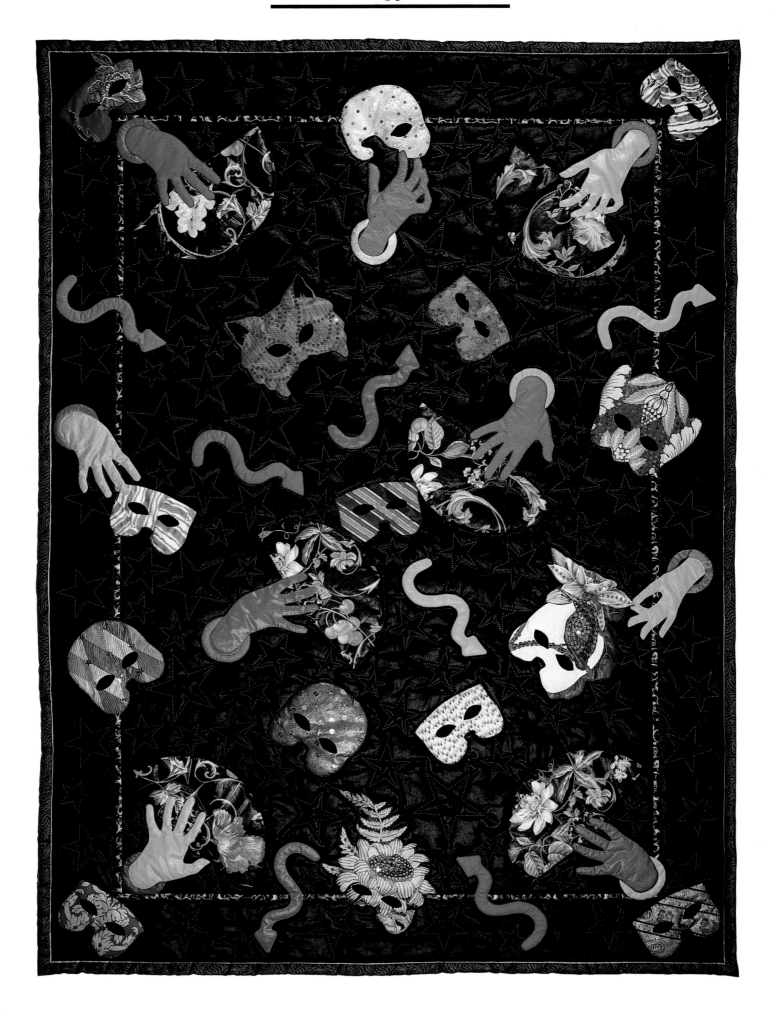

THE PROWLER
Sally Broadwell
Assorted fabrics, cotton backing, beads, feathers,
  rhinestones, found objects; machine piecing, hand
  applique, machine quilting
24"x 22", 1988
Collection of the artist

JUDY IN THE SKY
Sally Broadwell
Assorted fabrics, cotton backing, ribbon, paints, beads,
  found objects; machine piecing, hand applique,
  machine quilting
24"x 22", 1988
Collection of the artist

NIGHT MASQUE
"And pomp, and feast, and revelry,
With mask, and antique pageantry,
Such sights as youthful poets dream . . ."
  Milton, L'Allegro, (ll. 127-129)
Marjorie Claybrook
Cotton chintz, sateen, airbrush painted fabric, sequins,
  metallic threads for quilting; machine piecing for
  base, hand applique, hand quilting
75"x 55", 1990
Collection of the artist

SUSAN WEBB LEE

Another artist influenced by Crow is Susan Webb Lee. Like Crow, Lee designs directly on the wall and lets the piece develop from her interaction with the fabric before her, not from an existing drawing or plan. Her quilts exhibit her delight in color and fabric.

Lee began working with fabric after she took a course in surface design in graduate school. She was fascinated with the possiblities of working with fiber-reactive dyes. That, in turn, led her to wearable art and then quiltmaking as a way of using her hand-painted fabrics. Later, Lee turned to commercially dyed fabrics.

In "Poodle Quilt," (page 56) the viewer is struck by the tremendous variety of fabrics incorporated into the design. The artist has combined solids, plaids, and florals that, under another hand, might seem incongruous. Lee has pulled all these elements together to make a crisp, clean statement.

Her craftsmanship is impeccable and the work is the essence of control, but, even so, the rich variety of fabrics and interplay of color create strong dynamics and a tremendous sense of movement throughout the piece.

MARY JO DALRYMPLE

Mary Jo Dalrymple draws from a similarly wide assortment of fabric for her compositions. The quilt, "Barrier Gate," (page 57) incorporates Japanese ikat, silkscreened fabrics from Kenya, and a variety of hand-dyed and commerically produced cottons into the overall design. Dalrymple is able to combine these patterns and colors to create an inner light radiating from the center of the quilt. Her quilting is precise and effectively offsets the pieced design.

In writing about this work, Dalrymple quotes a definition of a barrier: "Anything, material or immaterial, that acts to obstruct or prevent passage." Here, solid colors of fabric seem to be "blocking" some of the printed or patterned fabrics she selected. We catch glimpses of clouds, leaves, and flowers walled within squares of fabric near the center of the quilt— near the source of light. These glimpses decrease with each border (or barrier) encountered, and finally entrance is achieved.

MURRAY JOHNSTON

Brilliant juxtapositions of color distinguish the work of Murray Johnston. Johnston effectively uses strip piecing to create the dynamic panels that make up "Midnight Conversations" (page 60). Deep and intense hues fill the front panels of the quilt. A few narrow bands of yellow glimmer across the surface. The limited use of this color creates a strong sense of movement in the overall design.

Small squares of black and white are pieced together in a checkerboard and form larger rectangular blocks, which appear at random throughout the quilt. Compounding this random quality are small white squares applied sparingly over the surface. These free-floating squares almost appear to have "chipped" off the larger blocks and add a buoyancy to the composition.

The quilt is made up of five individual hanging panels that overlap and are connected by a sleeve that runs across the back of each panel. Designed to be seen from both sides, the quilt offers two different moods, the front more vibrant and emotional than the back. The source of the composition, Johnston says, is her continuing interest in color and the way that it can communicate. "Through this communication in color we begin to have conversations with each other. . . . There is not

always an easy fluidity to it, there are many diagonals and conflicting directions as well as parts that float over the space and move across it. . . . The color emphasis (of the quilt) changes as you move around . . . . the way the tone of conversations change." Two striking red panels cut through the front three panels "disrupting" or "breaking" the conversational tone while the back panels, more subtle in color and hue, recede and project in their play of light and dark.

THE MYSTERY: AFTERNOON
Jane Burch Cochran
Various fabrics, canvas, acrylic paint, seed and bugle
    beads, buttons, jewelry; machine piecing, hand
    applique
35"x 45", 1987
Collection of the artist

UNWEARABLE ART SERIES: SOUVENIR SHIRT
Lynne Sward
Mixed cottons, found objects, plastic laminated
   photocopies; hand piecing, hand applique
24"x 24", 1990
Collection of the artist

SHARON HEIDINGSFELDER

Another artist who uses black and white fabric to great effect is Sharon Heidingsfelder. In "The Fat Lady Sings," (page 61) black and white squares and stripes are repeated throughout the pattern. Heidingsfelder says that she always uses black and white in her quilts because she likes the starkness against the colors.

Heidingsfelder has created a series of quilts related to music. She states that she is "intrigued with the rhythm of repeated patterns as well as with diverse color combinations. . . . I design my quilts by repeating a single block motif. Arranging and rearranging the blocks produces interesting shapes. After choosing one of the combinations, I then use strip-piecing, hand-dyed fabrics, or silkscreened prints to add more interest to some of the shapes." The quilting used by the artist augments the repetition of the blocks. In the "Fat Lady," closely-quilted circles and squares expand nicely upon the concept expressed by the pieced design.

MARJORIE CLAYBROOK

Black appears in many of these quilts as just one of several colors, but it is unusual to find a quilt, in this century or any other, that uses black as its primary color. Marjorie Claybrook, however, uses a black glossy surface as the stage for her mysterious "Night Masque" (page 64).

Masks, hands, and arrows in rich hues are applied to the black ground. Many of the masks are embellished with sequins, and the hands, expressive in their gestures and a powerful symbol in many cultures, lightly grasp a fan or mask. The artist's collection of masks, as well as Mardi Gras, were the inspirations for this piece. Carnival and its concurrent masquerades appeal to our desire for fantasy and mystery. Claybrook plays with these elements to create a piece with great theatricality. She enhances the applique designs with stars finely quilted in metallic thread.

SALLY BROADWELL

The process of embellishing or adding decoration to textile surfaces, quilts, or textiles in general, enjoys a long history. One artist who draws upon this tradition is Sally Broadwell. She has always been fascinated by historical and ethnic needlework, including Oriental embroideries, Persian rugs, and ecclesiastical vestments. "They invoke an emotional response," she says, "that I strive to recreate with the use of modern materials." Broadwell's diminutive and precisely executed work demands close inspection to fully appreciate the complexity of detail. She engages the viewer and brings him into these small worlds to explore and discover their hidden treasures.

In "The Prowler" and "Judy in the Sky" (page 65), Broadwell encrusted the surfaces with paints, beads, and found objects, including tiny plastic airplanes. She writes that the materials she uses are not precious, although they certainly try to be. In much of her recent work Broadwell is exploring light, either emitted from within the piece or reflected from the surface. "The inner light is implied and creates an illusion. The surface sparkle is real. It changes with movement and brings the image to life."

JANE BURCH COCHRAN

The work of Jane Burch Cochran exhibits a passion for beads, buttons and other articles applied as surface embellishment. Cochran was trained as a painter, made costume jewelry for a living, and collects beads. All three influences have come together in her fabric work. "The Mystery: Afternoon" (page 68) is one of a series of four pieces about creativity. This particular piece considers outside distractions. The black rectangle near the center, which Cochran identifies as an "adobe shape," represents the artist, while the snake and juggling hands represent temptations and distractions.

Cochran is inspired by American Indian beadwork and crazy quilts. "Crazy" patches of fabric are assembled around the central portion of the quilt. Cochran states that she "likes the uneven, random edge made from combining the stripped patches of cloth. I keep these edges (neat) by beading the pieces together rather than by hemming and appliqueing them." In addition to the beads and buttons, Cochran covered much of the surface with tiny dots of paint, echoing the bead and button forms.

She uses techniques and materials introduced into the quilt vocabulary during the last quarter of the 19th century in the form of crazy quilts. The difference between the 19th-century crazy quilts and the work of contemporary artists is the subject matter and the messages these objects convey to the viewer.

CIRCUS
Verena Levine
Cotton, poly-cotton, wool blends; machine piecing,
*   machine applique, hand quilting, embroidery*
58"x 68"
Collection of the artist

"DAY STAR" THE WINNER
Dorothy Holden
Ikat cotton, wool, silk oxford cloth, silk roses, sequins,
  men's socks; hand applique, hand quilting
56"x 61'', 1990
Collection of the artist

LYNNE SWARD

As more artists began exploring the possibilities of working with fabric, it was natural that "wearable art" would become part of the lexicon. Lynne Sward carries this idea to its natural, or unnatural, conclusion with her "Unwearable Art Series—Souvenir Shirt" (page 69). Living in Virginia Beach, Virginia, Sward is assaulted and inspired by the myriad of souvenir T-shirts available. She says the "fringe" technique used in the two-sided "Souvenir Shirt" originated in her clothing designs and, in addition, "illustrates the influence of American Indian ghost shirts and 'island grass-skirts' on my sense of creativity. I have been exploring 'clothes' (the image) as a design source for many years."

The combination of color, variety of printed fabrics and the way the shirt has been assembled testify to Sward's interest in color and texture. Making a shirt about a shirt illustrates her sense of satire and indebtedness to popular culture. Incorporated into the design are postcards, plastic toys, and beach souvenirs. Sward says that "this affordable and informal article of clothing is well-suited to most homogeneous and economic groups all over the world. It is with respect and humor that I pay homage to a true American icon."

VERENA LEVINE

In addition to exploring formal aspects of color, light, and spatial relationships, artists in fiber are working in narrative and figurative styles. Among them is Verena Levine, whose work often depicts childhood memories with the charm and spontaneity exhibited in some folk art.

Levine began painting as a teenager growing up in Switzerland and continued during her years of training and work as a medical technologist. In 1973 Levine's husband took a position in Bangladesh where Levine had difficulty acquiring paper for her work. However, beautiful fabrics were abundant and she began making her pictures out of the rich variety of material her temporary home offered. After returning to the United States, Levine never returned to paint and paper. "I like the built-in patterns and textures of the fabrics."

In "Circus," (page 72) she began with a small drawing and then pieced a background and applied animals and figures that capture the feeling of the circus coming to a small community. The fabrics are remarkably appropriate to her composition. Her depictions of people and animals are simple and direct, allowing her to illustrate the essence of the characters in her story. The animals take center stage and are engaging and whimsical.

DOROTHY HOLDEN

Dorothy Holden joins Levine in creating an animal with charm and personality. " 'Daystar' The Winner" (page 73) is a large horse made from mates to socks that never returned from the laundry (where do those socks go?). Holden arranged the socks, uncut, on a background fabric of cotton ikat.

The socks take on the persona of the horse and assume an anthropomorphic quality. The body has a great sense of movement making the viewer feel that the roses around his neck are most deserved. Holden, like many other contemporary quilters, does not have any set rules dictating what can and cannot be incorporated into the quilt. This openness to various materials and techniques allows the artist's personal expression the latitude to blossom.

Holden's work varies from the figurative, like "Daystar," to abstract quilt designs, but she is becoming best known for her quilted portraits. The first portrait she made was of herself and she has received several commissions for others. The portraits begin as "Daystar" did, a drawing on a piece of paper (often a grocery bag), which are then transferred to cloth. Her imaginative representations effectively capture her subjects.

TERESA TUCKER YOUNG

Continuing the narrative theme is Teresa Tucker Young with her quilt, "Manhattan Maidens/Having It All" (page 76). Young tackles the myth of the "superwoman" who can do it all—career, marriage, children, exercise—and keep her sanity. She uses Manhattan as the setting (although this story takes place everywhere) since it most glorifies the fast-paced, high-pressure existence Young wanted to illustrate. Young says she was also drawn to the yellow taxicabs and wanted to use them in a piece.

Young often works with the female figure, but the women in this quilt have greater depth and dimension than those in some of her other work. The background of this piece is also more developed and integrated with the figures in the foreground. The central figure is the blue lady on the phone, and she is surrounded by her other selves—the bride in a Cinderella-type dress, mother-to-be, and exercise fiend. Around her are clocks, reminding her that time is slipping away and that no matter how fast she runs she will not win this race. There are references, as well, to woman's biological clock.

Young's piece, with its careful layering and quilting, is painterly, but its wonderful tactile quality reminds the viewer why artists like Young choose fabric over paint. To them, the softness and plasticity of fabric are not offered by paint.

MANHATTAN MAIDENS / HAVING IT ALL
Teresa Tucker Young
Cotton, poly-cotton; hand piecing, hand applique,
  embroidery, hand quilting
60"x 60", 1990
Collection of the artist

**MY ANCESTRESS DANCED (THE WORLD
INTO BEING)**
Patricia Maimon-Music
Silk, cotton, velvet, antique silk, metallic fabrics; hand
  piecing, hand quilting
89"x 56", 1989
Collection of the artist

PATRICIA MAIMON-MUSIC

Another artist exploring the human form with understanding and obvious pleasure is Patricia Maimon-Music. In "My Ancestress Danced (The World Into Being)" (page 77), Maimon-Music creates a very large female figure who is moving, dancing, with enormous power and force. The body is composed of a variety of rich fabrics—velveteen, silks, and metallics—but its power is derived chiefly from the quilting.

The figure's legs are heavily quilted, giving the thighs and calves tremendous muscularity. The face is elusive. Cloud-like quilted stitches obscure and then reveal. We almost see the face, then, as if covered by a cloud or reflected in a distant pool, it is gone. Hexagonal-shaped pieces extend from the neck down the entire length of the body like vertebrae. By including antique silks and exotic fabrics, she creates a sense of the universality of her representation as an ancestor for us all. No one culture can be identified with this figure.

JIMMIE BENEDICT

Landscape is a theme represented in the work of many artists living in the South. While Wilchins and Whittington observe their immediate environment, Jimmie Benedict takes the desert of the Southwest as her inspiration. In "Georgia On My Mind, Big" (page 80), Benedict pays homage to Georgia O'Keeffe and expresses her love of the area of New Mexico where O'Keeffe lived and worked for many years.

Benedict often works with the triangle as she explores color relationships. As she tells it, "Many of Georgia O'Keeffe's paintings or pieces of paintings pushed their way onto this large screen form . . . a pebble, big. Most recognizable are the mountain Pedernal, the Red Poppy, the Cliffs Above Abiquiu, and the pelvis form. They are combined with my pyramid sky and soft shapes. I have selected a screen so that my (quilt) . . . . could be viewed from all sides. . . . This is the first [screen I have made] on this scale."

Benedict's work glows and vibrates. The optical play of colors in the sky is an effective backdrop for the cliffs and is evocative of the light and colors of the Southwestern sky. The free-standing screen format allows the viewer to follow the sensual form of the poppy as it reappears on the obverse, this time in concert with triangles in black and white.

SUSAN HARLAN

Many of the quilts made by Susan Harlan illustrate her celebration of nature and her interest in "growing things." Look At These Now" (page 81) is one a series of bird quilts that Harlan says are inspired by her garden, the bird feeder outside her studio window and 19th-century naturalist, John James Audubon.

The first impression when looking at this quilt, however, is not the actual representation of nature and birds, but the strong abstract quality of its design. Harlan's eye-popping colors and formal arrangement of the figures create life and movement on the quilt surface. The glazed chintzes reflect light and add to the overall dynamics. The inclusion of printed fabrics in this quilt was new for Harlan who in the past has restricted herself to solid colors or all white. Harlan has machine quilted the top onto polyurethane foam, enhancing the depth and dimension she is able to achieve in the quilt surface.

BERNIE ROWELL

Bernie Rowell also takes pleasure in making connections with the world around her, whether it is cast off "trash" from our industrial culture, elements of which inspired her "Urban Icons" series, or infrared photographs of Earth. Rowell has observed, "From the vantage point of space, man's imprint of the earth's surface is distinctly geometric. Infrared photography reveals the asphalt grids of inner cities, the spider webs of suburban streets, patchwork farms laid out by the acre. I was struck by how closely the elements in these photographs related to the visual language in my own artwork. The woven grids, the basic geometric forms, the stitched linear drawings all lend themselves to interpreting these earth views."

"Inside Out—Aerial View Series 1990" (page 84) is a beautiful interpretation of these relationships. As with the natural world, our perceptions of the land from above and how it actually exists below are called into question when studying Rowell's piece. From a distance we are soothed by the gentle gradations of color as our eye moves easily over the intricately worked surface. Closer examination reveals the multitude of little worlds that exist on the surface. Dots of paint, fringed canvas, pleating, and cut embroidery are some of the elements which create the surface depth and interest. The peaceful canvas seen from a distance is in actuality a complex network of interrelationships.

GEORGIA ON MY MIND, BIG
Jimmie L. Benedict
Cotton, silk, poly-moiré taffeta, acetate taffeta; machine
    piecing, machine applique, machine quilting,
    embroidery, drawing
60"x 78", 1990
Collection of the artist
Photograph by David Luttrell

LOOK AT THESE NOW II
Susan Harlan
*Chintz and other printed fabrics; machine quilting onto
    polyurethane foam*
50"x 52", 1990
Collection of the artist

ELLEN ZAHOREC

Like Bernie Rowell, Ellen Zahorec uses stitched canvas to create her work. At first, one is almost overwhelmed by the riot of color in "Parallelogram Diptych" (page 85), but the structure of the grid and the repetitive shapes keep the feeling of control in the midst of all the exuberance. Zahorec developed the idea for this piece out of a fascination for the reverse side of quilts and the "need to see the 'ugly' side of a beautiful piece."

The machine-stitched squares of canvas are filled with X-es, O-s, and triangles in a variety of colors. Other artists have employed this grid format, filling the squares with their personal symbols. Zahorec's work, however, relates more closely, visually, to Eastern European and Indian embroidery styles. The intensely-colored panels are full of life and offer the visual equivalent to Zahorec's exhortations written on the upper right panel: "Let's work to create as much beauty as possible." She has also written, "It's o.k. if I'm scared I found out that the boogie man is just a scare tactic," and "Who knows exactly what is going on with (the) world. We just have to do our best."

STEPHANIE SANTMYERS

Stephanie Santmyers puts her great technical skill to work exploring illusion and spacial relationships. "Sister Ship" (page 88) is one of a series of space quilts that grew out of her interest in science fiction and space exploration. Our sense of depth and dimensionality are put to work in ascertaining the relationships of various forms and shapes in the quilt.

In the center of the quilt is a large egg-like shape, which is cut from a fabric with an organic feeling; it contrasts with the more rigid, high-tech quality imparted by the solids and stripes. Santmyers sketches her idea first in graphite and black ink. Then she masterfully translates these black and white shadows and illusions into fabric, creating various visual depths.

VERONICA FITZGERALD

Veronica Fitzgerald machine pieces enormous quilts, usually 80 to 100 inches in one direction, with great bold strokes of color and form. Upon the striking surface of "Yucatan" (page 89) Fitzgerald applied narrow silk ribbons in repetitive lines that run down the quilt surface in sharp zig-zags. She felt the finished quilt "needed something to hold it together" and conceived of the ribbons to provide the anchor.

Fitzgerald cites traditional quilts as an influence in her work as well as her profession (she works as a biochemist). A few years ago while pursuing a degree in art, she began noticing quilts and decided to use them as her vehicle for self-expression. Much of the excitement in Fitzgerald's work comes from the impact of the quilt size and pattern combined with the delicacy of surface detail. It is possible to relate the two elements to two aspects of Fitzgerald's life: the world at large and the world under a microscope. Both must influence her vision.

Fitzgerald states that quiltmaking is "my way of inventing, discovering and solving problems. My eye is constantly searching for a new way to use an old pattern; for a more expressive color combination; for just the right juxtaposition of patterned fabrics; for an image that speaks. Tedium is interspersed with joy. Ultimate gratification comes when I see the finished quilt."

GEORGIA SPRINGER

An artist who has channeled her vision into incredibly small worlds is Georgia Springer. Springer has been sewing since she was four years old, and for a number of years making quilts that explore color, light and space. "Recently, I have been interested in incorporating actual light into my work through the use of transparent materials which allow me to go beyond mere visual reproduction of the effects of light."

Springer's new work, "Reverse Solutions" (page 92) is taken from a passage in *Daybook* by artist Ann Truitt. Truitt tells of finding solutions to problems by trying the opposite, or reversing the obvious. Springer explains that for her, this meant making very small pieces, using hard transparent materials and unraveling, pulling apart fibers and fabric instead of stitching them together.

In this series of five works Springer incorporates various transparent and opaque materials. Two works in the series, "Menominee" and "That Time Then" (page 92) were influenced by childhood memories of her midwestern landscape and the attempt to capture moments of remembered color and light. The pieces are ethereal, and the delicate fibers seem to dance and swirl within their transparent casings. The effect of movement echoes some of Springer's earlier quilts, but the added transparency enhances that effect. These new materials have changed Springer's work and allow her to explore other issues. However, she has retained the idea of layering and recomposing cut up scraps and fragments into what she calls a "new visual reality. This collage aspect of my work is akin to the patchwork process."

INSIDE OUT—AERIAL VIEW SERIES
Bernie Rowell
Canvas, mesh, acrylic paints, metallic fabrics and
*   threads; machine applique, machine line drawings,*
*   pleating, cut embroidery*
52"x 92", 1990
Collection of the artist

PARALLELOGRAM DIPTYCH
Ellen Zahorec
Primed canvas, acrylic and enamel paint, corduroy
    backing; machine piecing
84"x 96", 1990
Collection of the artist

ARTURO ALONZO SANDOVAL

Arturo Alonzo Sandoval uses a variety of materials beyond fiber. "What distinguishes me from other artists working in fiber is my choice to mainly explore 20th-century industrial materials." The materials work well with his design concepts, which more recently focus on domestic and social issues, international terrorism and nuclear war.

Sandoval finds the surfaces created through the use of high-tech materials exciting. Mylars, microfilm, and fabric combine with photography and Xerox transfers to make images that are at once abstract and representational and surfaces with reflections that provide an added dimension to the final work. Sandoval says he chose textiles for the focus of his creative energies because he was excited by the "variety of expression and abstraction that you could get in a pattern. Textile design brought immediate results and it was very expressive."

"Heritage Festival Faces: Windows of Creativity" (page 92) is made from the industrial materials Sandoval prefers and was partially funded by the Lexington, Kentucky Community Arts Program to produce a community impact artwork. As Sandoval explains the process, "Color Polaroids were taken of each participant (of Arts Heritage Week in Lexington) . . . . the portrait blocks were made six at a time on a copy machine on acetate transparencies. The transparencies

were stitched together into seven panels which are then stitched to various colored Mylars, veiling, pelon, and paper. Transparent thread holds all of the layers together and allows all of the portraits to remain visible. These pieces are fragile. . . . therefore I apply a fabric backing to these plastic materials."

Sandoval's repeated use of the triangle in colors of red, blue, sepia, and black moves our eye over the composition and adds a traditional quality to the piece. A quotation from Allen Eaton's book, *The Handicrafts of the Southern Highlands*, is repeated across the surface of the work: "He who does creative work, whether he dwell in a palace or in a hut, has in his house a window through which he may look out upon some of life's finest scenes."

In this sentence, Eaton extolled both the virtues and rewards of creating. Eaton also wrote that one day we will judge work by two measurements: "one by the product itself, as is now done, the other by the effect of the work on the producer." In his definition of art Eaton includes "even the lowliest of tasks (which) have been done beautifully . . . . It becomes clear to him (the producer) that it is not what one does that determines a work of art but the manner in which it is done." This concept, in concert with the faces on Sandoval's quilt, is a prod for the democratization of art-making. It reflects Sandoval's social concerns just as much as it does his interest in color and form.

BRUCE BOBICK

Another artist expressing his concern for contemporary society is Bruce Bobick. "Ceremonial Shroud" (page 93) is a continuation of a series of "recently unearthed artifacts" from an imaginary white culture living in North America before the American Indians, a culture Bobick calls the Annimar.

Bobick created an elaborate series of myths, structure, and history of the society, numerous "excavated" objects (primarily of paper, stone, and various fibers) and theories expressed by archeologists and psychologists interpreting his imaginary society. The objects, with detailed information accompanying each piece, were exhibited in a museum of history. In spite of the show's title, which stated that the Annimar was an imaginary culture, the society and the pieces assumed a reality.

Bobick calls the series "an attempt to create a rational, utopian society as a reaction to the knowledge that we live in a world in which violence and death are integral parts." The Annimar are described as a non-violent, agrarian people who obviously created beautiful objects and represent a type of ideal human community.

Bobick explores the workings of the subconscious mind. Realizing that the subconscious mind is active during sleep, he previously created a series of watercolors of quilts made by the grandmothers of such creative geniuses as Nicolaus Copernicus, Eli Whitney, Edgar Allen Poe, and Amelia Earhart. "The quilts, used on the beds (of these people) during their formative years, contain visual images which permeated the subconscious night after night and thus led directly to the famous invention, discovery, or work of art."

After the quilt project, Bobick, who considers himself a painter who sometimes uses other materials to express himself, became aware of the "expressive potential" fabric held for him. In the case of "Ceremonial Shroud" (page 93), Bobick did all of the sewing himself.

With his unusual intellectual curiosity, Bobick looks at history and people from an angle different from most of us. His musings are sometimes humorous, and always provocative. The speculations on the Annimar urge us to confront the violence and inhumanity that is part of our culture.

SISTER SHIP
Stephanie Santmyers
Cotton, poly-cotton, ribbon; machine piecing, hand
  applique, hand quilting
57"x 60", 1990
Collection of the artist

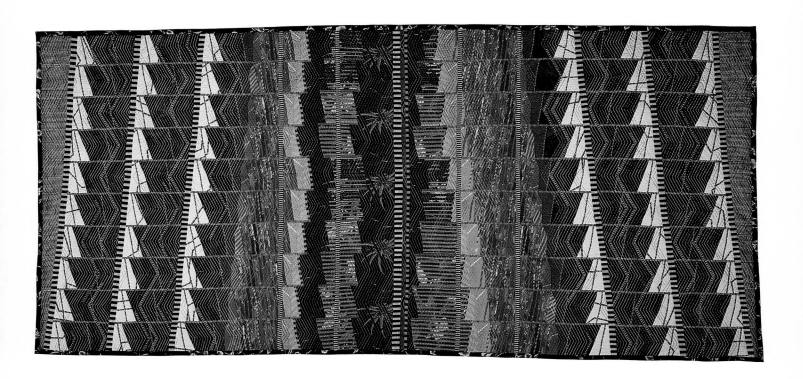

YUCATAN
Veronica Fitzgerald
Silk and cotton; machine piecing, hand quilting
85"x 168", 1986
Collection of the artist

VOICES OF THE SOUTH

The artists in this collection are all working in the South. Many were reared here and thus share some sensibilities stemming from attachment to the region. Much criticism today in art and literature focuses on regional similarities and differences. Critics and historians try to define a specific style or voice emanating from a particular area of the country. Quilt historians have had some success with this pursuit in the area of antique quilts, and we can now point to some areas of common ground in contemporary quiltmaking as well.

Quiltmaking contines to be an active tradition in the South, and many of the artists shown in this collection are working from a background of family or community-based knowledge of quiltmaking or sewing. Jimmie Benedict writes that fabrics and quilting have always been a part of her life. "My grandmother was a quilter, my other grandmother and mother sewed for a living. My sisters and I come by it very naturally. Come to think of it my brother sews too. I do not consider myself a traditional quilter, but I express my thoughts or designs in fabric. . . .and put a batting in them. I guess that makes me a quilter." Bernie Rowell states that she has always been a sewer "so one tends to build on existing skills because they are comfortable."

Artists who work in fiber, however, are aware of, and most have felt, the prejudice sometimes expressed for the medium. Sue Alvarez has been a quilter for 18 years but has sewed since she was ten. "My grandmother asked me what I wanted to be when I grew up and I said I just wanted to sew. 'You have to pick again,' she said!"

Artists state that because the medium is female oriented and involves non-precious materials, some people hesitate to invest in something that "only" has women's time. The medium does not hold enough mystery for some. Despite such negatives most studio artists feel buoyed by the current enthusiasm for the studio quilt and feel this enthusiasm is removing the "women's work" stigma—at least from the contemporary quilt.

One element that binds the work of many contemporary Southern quilters, painters, writers, and other artists is their love of their landscape. The evidence is often overtly expressed in the design, as in the work of Nancy Whittington and Nancy Harlan. Sometimes the inspiration is less obvious and may be expressed through explorations of color and light as in the work of Bernie Rowell.

Although some artists acknowledge feelings of isolation, working away from centers considered "artistic mainstreams," they value the concentration that solitude can bring. When they do meet with other artists (within and out of fabric), they feel very much a part of that network and appreciate the support it gives them.

Many of the artists in this survey feel passionate about fabric. It is a necessary part of their expression. Others use fabric as they would any other materials; it just happens to be the medium they are using to explore and express their concerns at any given time.

Fabric often broadens the avenue of expression. As Jane Burch Cochran says, "My art quilts are an eclectic joining of my various art experiences. . . . I unconsciously combine the loose, free feeling of abstract painting with the time-consuming and controlled techniques of beading and sewing. . . . I feel liberated to expand my visual vocabulary from just paint to include cloth, beads, thread [and] buttons."

Susan Harlan says a factor influencing her to become a quilt artist was that she wanted to "work *big*." She also says that she chose the quilt because it is "a mirror of the American consciousness. . . . There is a sensual beauty and permanent quality to the American quilt tradition which I want to celebrate and to preserve for future generations.''

Murray Johnston also appreciates quilt history, and she wants to expand upon that vocabulary. ''The women making quilts 100 years ago were attempting to create something of beauty in often harsh surroundings. They made quilts that related to their world and I want to continue that tradition by making quilts that relate to my world.''

Most of the artists in this exhibition, being women, appreciate the long history of women in the needle arts. Sally Broadwell feels that her work ''exemplifies that which women have been creating throughout history. They have used the materials available to them and have carried out the human need to embellish and beautify. My work contains the subtleties, tedium and pride in workmanship that is the core of women's work.''

Georgia Springer says that ''the themes weaving back and forth in my work over the years involve my identity as a woman, my relationship with my physical surroundings and the making of a visual reality of my inner world—all longtime concerns of quiltmakers.'' Elizabeth Cherry Owen states that she continues to be ''drawn to fabric and the traditional methods of quiltmaking because they are familiar and emotionally accessible both to the viewer and the maker.''

Other artists, such as Patsy Allen, Arturo Sandoval and Bruce Bobick, do not feel the same type of attachment to the history of quiltmaking or to the use of fabric. They feel they are using the materials appropriate to their expression. Their view is best expressed by Ellen Zahorec: ''Quilting alone means nothing to me. . . . but creating means everything!!!! Any medium or material is the artist's just tool for creation and expression— whether it be stitchery, quilting or painting— the need to communicate and reveal oneself is of utmost importance.''

The studio quilt movement has arrived at an exciting juncture in the South. As more artists discover the potential of working with fabric more viewers are coming to accept the contemporary nature of the creations. They see that studio quilt artists are not negating the tradition of the quilt, but rather building on the past and expanding the form. Most artists possess a sense of history and an appreciation for the traditions associated with quilts as well as the special qualities of cloth. To them cloth has a dual nature of ordinariness and mystery. Its power derives from its everyday uses and associations with life's most important rites and rituals. Artists are able to draw upon these associations and create works expressing them.

In their studio quilts, artists also reveal regard for nature and landscape, spirituality, and freedom of expression. Their standards of excellence are evidenced by the high quality of craftsmanship.

Departures from the time-honored quilt form and function simultaneously stimulate our senses and deepen our appreciation of the old form. Southern artists, by expressing their concerns and inquiries in new forms, are adding to a most venerable tradition and keeping it fresh and new.

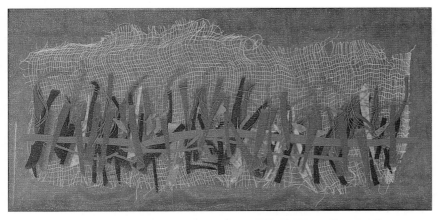

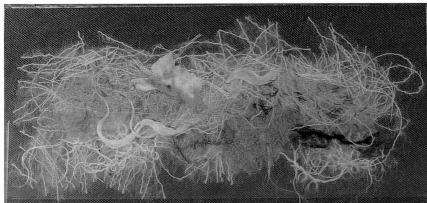

**REVERSE SOLUTIONS SERIES
MENONIMEE
THAT TIME THEN**
Georgia Springer
Glass, fiber, plastic, metal, Plexiglas base
5"x 10"x 3/16", 1989
Collection of the artist

**HERITAGE FESTIVAL FACES: WINDOWS
OF CREATIVITY**
Arturo Sandoval
*Fiber mixed media, mylar, acetate transparencies,
    monofilament threads, paper, netting, paint, canvas
    backing, velcro/wood supports; machine stitching,
    machine piecing*
88"x 224", 1989
Collection of the artist — Funded in part by the Lexington, Kentucky
Fund for the Arts, Community Arts Development Program

CEREMONIAL SHROUD
Bruce Bobick
*Animal hides, bones and skulls, raw cotton, linen; hand
    piecing*
101"x 50", 1990
Collection of Art Space, Atlanta, Georgia

List of Artists and Their Works

Patsy Allen, Greensboro, NC, *Threshold III*

Sue Alvarez, Fries, VA, *Beach Games*

Jimmie Benedict, Knoxville, TN,
Georgia on My Mind, Big

Bruce Bobick, Carrollton, GA,
Ceremonial Shroud

Sally Broadwell, St. Augustine, FL,
The Prowler, Judy in the Sky

Marjorie Claybrook, Augusta, GA,
Night Masque

Jane Burch Cochran, Rabbit Hash, KY,
The Mystery; Afternoon

Mary Jo Dalrymple, Omaha, NE,
Barrier Gate

Lenore Davis, Newport, KY,
The Small City

Veronica Fitzgerald, Andersonville, TN,
Yucatan

Susan Harlan, Atlanta, GA,
Look At These Now II

Sharon Heidingsfelder, Little Rock, AR,
The Fat Lady Sings

Dorothy Holden, Charlottesville, VA,
"Daystar" The Winner

Murray Johnston, Birmingham, AL,
Midnight Conversations

Ellen Kochansky, Pickens, SC,
Volcanic Activity

Susan Webb Lee, Greensboro, NC,
Poodle Quilt

Verena Levine, Durham, NC,
Circus

Patricia Maimon-Music, Atlanta, GA,
*My Ancestress Danced (The World
Into Being)*

Elizabeth Cherry Owen, Baton Rouge, LA,
Tennessee Waltz

Bernie Rowell, Knoxville, TN,
Inside Out—Aerial View Series

Arturo Alonzo Sandoval, Lexington, KY,
*Heritage Festival Faces: Windows of
Creativity*

Stephanie Santmyers, Greensboro, NC,
Sister Ship

Georgia Springer, Raleigh, NC,
Menominee, That Time Then

Lynne Sward, Virginia Beach, VA,
Unwearable Art Series: Souvenir Shirt

Nancy Whittington, Carrboro, NC,
Leaf Symmetry III

Susan Wilchins, Raleigh, NC,
Night Thoughts II

Teresa Tucker Young, Georgetown, KY,
Manhattan Maidens/Having It All

Ellen Zahorec, Brevard, NC,
Parallelogram Diptych

Bibliography

ACKLAND ART MUSEUM. *North Carolina Country Quilts: Regional Variations.* Chapel Hill: Ackland Art Museum, University of North Carolina at Chapel Hill, 1979.

AMERICAN CRAFT MUSEUM. See Museum of Contemporary Crafts.

BEER, ALICE BALDWIN. *Trade Goods.* Washington, District of Columbia: Smithsonian Institution Press, 1970.

BIRMINGHAM MUSEUM OF ART. *Black Belt to Hill Country: Alabama Quilts from the Robert and Helen Cargo Collection.* Birmingham, Alabama: Birmingham Museum of Art, 1982.

BRACKMAN, BARBARA. *Clues in the Calico: A Guide to Identifying and Dating Antique Quilts.* McLean, Virginia: EPM Publications, 1989.

BULLARD, LUCY FOLMAR, and BETTY JO SHIELL. *Chintz Quilts: Unfading Glory.* Tallahassee, Florida: Serendipity Publishers, 1983.

BURDICK, NANCILU B. *Legacy: The Story of Talula Gilbert Bottoms and Her Quilts.* Nashville, Tennessee: Rutledge Hill Press, 1988.

CALLAHAN, NANCY. " 'Helping the Peoples To Help Themselves'." *The Quilt Digest 4* (1986): 20–29.
—. *The Freedom Quilting Bee.* Tuscaloosa: University of Alabama Press, 1987.

CARGO, ROBERT T. "Long Remembered: An Alabama Pioneer and Her Quilts." *The Quilt Digest 3* (1985): 60–69.

CLARKE, MARY WASHINGTON. *Kentucky Quilts and Their Makers.* Lexington: The University Press of Kentucky, 1976.

—. *Clothing and Textiles in the Nineteenth-Century South.* Special issue of *Southern Quarterly*, vol. 27, no. 1 (Fall 1988). Hattiesburg, Mississippi: University of Southern Mississippi.

COLBY, AVERIL. *Patchwork.* London: B. T. Batsford, 1958.
—. *Patchwork Quilts.* London: B. T. Batsford, 1965.

COUNTS, CHARLES, ED. *Pieceworks 2.* Gainesville, Georgia: Georgia Mountain Crafts, 1987.

CROW, NANCY. *Quilts and Influences.* Paducah, Kentucky: American Quilter's Society, 1990.

DAR MUSEUM. *Old Line Traditions: Maryland Women and Their Quilts.* Washington, District of Columbia: DAR Museum, 1985.

DAVIS, DAVID BRION. *The Problem of Slavery in the Age of the Revolution 1770–1823.* Ithaca, New York: Cornell University Press, 1975.

DeCORDOVA MUSEUM. *Bed and Board: Contemporary Quilts and Woodwork.* Lincoln, Massachusetts: DeCordova Museum, 1975.

DUBERMAN, MARTIN. *Black Mountain: An Experiment in Community:* New York: E. P. Dutton, 1972.

EATON, ALLEN. *Handicrafts of the Southern Highlands.* New York: Russell Sage Foundation, 1937.

FERRERO, PAT, ELAINE HEDGES, AND JULIE SILBER. *Hearts and Hands: The Influence of Women & Quilts on American Society.* San Francisco: The Quilt Digest Press, 1987.

FERRIS, WILLIAM, ED. *Afro-American Folk Arts and Crafts.* Jackson: University Press of Mississippi, 1983.

FINLEY, RUTH E. *Old Patchwork Quilts and the Women Who Made Them.* New York: Grosset and Dunlap, 1929.

FOX-GENOVESE, ELIZABETH. *Within the Plantation Household: Black and White Women of the Old South.* Chapel Hill: University of North Carolina Press, 1988.

FREEMAN, RONALD. *Something To Keep You Warm.* Jackson: Mississippi Department of Archives and History, 1981.

FRENCH, LUCY VIRGINIA SMITH. *War Journal 1860-1865,* typescript. Nashville, Tennessee: State Library and Archives.

GAROUTTE, SALLY. "Marseilles Quilts and Their Woven Offspring." *Uncoverings 1982.* Mill Valley, California: American Quilt Study Group, 1983, 115–134.
—. "Early Colonial Quilts in a Bedding Context." *Uncoverings 1980.* Mill Valley, California: American Quilt Study Group, 1981, 18–27.

GOUMA-PETERSON, THALIA. *Miriam Schapiro: A Retrospective. 1953-1980.* Wooster, Ohio: College of Wooster, 1980.

GREAT AMERICAN GALLERY. *Americana Enshrined.* Atlanta, Georgia: Great American Gallery, 1989.

GUNN, VIRGINIA. "Quilts at Nineteenth Century State and County Fairs: An Ohio Study." *Uncoverings 1988.* San Francisco: American Quilt Study Group, 1989, 105–128.

HARNEY, ANDY LEON. "WPA Handicrafts Rediscovered." *Historic Preservation.* (July 1973): 10–15.

HENLEY, BRYDING ADAMS. "Alabama Gunboat Quilts." *Uncoverings 1987.* San Francisco: American Quilt Study Group, 1989, 11–23.

HOLSTEIN, JONATHAN. *The Pieced Quilt: An American Design Tradition.* Greenwich, Connecticut: New York Graphic Society, 1973.

HORTON, LAUREL. *Glorified Patchwork: South Carolina Crazy Quilts.* Columbia: McKissick Museum, University of South Carolina, 1989.
—. "South Carolina Quilts and the Civil War." *Uncoverings 1985.* Mill Valley, California: American Quilt Study Group, 1986, 53–70.
—. "South Carolina's Traditional Quilts." *Uncoverings 1984.* Mill Valley, California: American Quilt Study Group, 1985, 55–70.
—. "The Textile Industry and South Carolina Quilts." *Uncoverings 1988.* San Francisco: American Quilt Study Group, 1989, 129–150.

HORTON, LAUREL, AND LYNN MYERS. *Social Fabric: South Carolina's Traditional Quilts.* Columbia: McKissick Museum, University of South Carolina, 1985.

HUNTER MUSEUM OF ART. *New Quilts of the Mid-South.* Chattanooga, Tennessee: Hunter Museum of Art, 1986.
—. *Quilt Close-up: Five Southern Views.* Chattanooga, Tennessee: Hunter Museum of Art, 1983.

JAMES, MICHAEL. "Beyond Tradition: The Art of the Studio Quilt." *American Craft.* vol. 45, no. 1 (Feb./March 1985): 18–22.

KATZENBURG, DENA. *Baltimore Album Quilts.* Baltimore: Baltimore Museum of Art, 1981.

KENDRICK, A. F. *English Needlework.* 1933. 2nd ed. revised by Patricia Wardle. London: Adam & Charles Black, 1967.

KENTUCKY QUILT PROJECT. *Kentucky Quilts 1800–1900.* Louisville: Kentucky Quilt Project, Inc., 1982.

KIRKPATRICK, ERMA H. "A Study of 'Alamance Plaids' and Their Use in North Carolina Quilts." *Uncoverings 1988.* San Francisco: American Quilt Study Group, 1989, 45–56.
—. "Quilts, Quiltmaking, and the *Progressive Farmer,* 1886–1935." *Uncoverings 1985.* Mill Valley, California: American Quilt Study Group, 1986, 137–146.

LOHRENZ, MARY EDNA, AND ANITA MILLER STAMPER. *Mississippi Homespun: Nineteenth Century Textiles and the Women Who Made Them.* Jackson: Mississippi Department of Archives and History, 1989.

McMORRIS, PENNY. *Crazy Quilts.* New York: E. P. Dutton, 1984.

McMORRIS, PENNY, AND MICHAEL KILE. *The Art Quilt.* San Francisco: Quilt Digest Press, 1986.

MANHART, MARCIA, AND TOM MANHART, EDS. *The Eloquent Object.* Tulsa, Oklahoma: Philbrook Museum of Art, 1987.

MEYER, SUELLEN. "Early Influences of the Sewing Machine and Visible Machine Stitching on Nineteenth-Century Quilts." *Uncoverings 1989.* San Francisco: American Quilt Study Group, 1990, 38–53.

MONTGOMERY, FLORENCE M. *Textiles in America 1650–1870.* New York: W. W. Norton, 1984.

MURRELL, EMILY. Diary, 1850. Photocopy. Nashville, Tennessee: State Library and Archives.

MUSEUM OF CONTEMPORARY CRAFTS [NOW AMERICAN CRAFT MUSEUM]. *The New American Quilt.* New York: Museum of Contemporary Crafts, 1976.

NICKOLS, PAT L. "The Use of Cotton Sacks in Quiltmaking." *Uncoverings 1988.* San Francisco: American Quilt Study Group, 1989, 57–72.

ORLOFSKY, PATSY AND MYRON. *Quilts in America.* New York: McGraw Hill, 1974.

PETO, FLORENCE. *American Quilts and Coverlets.* New York: Chanticleer Press, 1949.
—. *Historical Quilts.* New York: The American Historical Company, 1939.

PETTIT, FLORENCE H. *America's Printed and Painted Fabrics.* New York: Hastings House, 1970.

QUILT NATIONAL. *New Quilts: Interpretations and Innovations.* Exton, Pennsylvania: Schiffer Publishing, 1989.
—. *Quilts: The State of An Art.* Exton, Pennsylvania: Schiffer Publishing, 1985.
—. *The Quilt: New Directions for an American Tradition.* Exton, Pennsylvania: Schiffer Publishing, 1983.

RAMSEY, BETS. "Cotton Country: Redbud, Georgia 1873–1907." *Quilt Close-up: Five Southern Views.* Chattanooga, Tennessee: Hunter Museum of Art, 1983, 18–27.
—. *Old & New Quilt Patterns in the Southern Tradition.* Nashville, Tennessee: Rutledge Hill Press, 1987.
—. "The Land of Cotton: Quiltmaking by African-American Women in Three Southern States." *Uncoverings 1988.* San Francisco: American Quilt Study Group, 1989, 9–28.

RAMSEY, BETS, AND MERIKAY WALDVOGEL. *The Quilts of Tennessee: Images of Domestic Life Prior to 1930.* Nashville, Tennessee: Rutledge Hill Press, 1986.

ROBERSON, RUTH, ED. *North Carolina Quilts.* Chapel Hill: University of North Carolina Press, 1988.

SAFFORD, CARLETON L., AND ROBERT BISHOP. *America's Quilts and Coverlets.* New York: E. P. Dutton, 1972.

SMITH, PAUL, AND EDWARD LUCIE-SMITH. *Craft Today: Poetry of the Physical.* New York: Weidenfeld and Nicholson, 1986.

STEINBAUM, BERNICE, ED. *The Definitive Contemporary American Quilt.* New York: Bernice Steinbaum Gallery, 1990.

TIMBY, DEBORAH BIRD, ED. *Visions: Quilts of a New Decade.* Lafayette, California: C & T Publishing, 1990.

TRECHSEL, GAIL ANDREWS. "Nineteenth-Century Chintz Quilts." *Southern Accents* (Mar./April 1989)
—. "Quiltmaking." *Alabama Folklife: Collected Essays.* Ed. Stephen H. Martin, Birmingham, Alabama: Alabama Folk Association, 1989, 22–27.
—. Review of *Americana Enshrined. Arts Journal* (Nov. 1989): 18–19.

VICTORIA & ALBERT MUSEUM. *Fifty Masterpieces of Textiles.* London: Her Majesty's Stationery Office, 1951.

WAHLMAN, MAUDE. "Aesthetic Principles." *Afro-American Folk Art and Crafts.* Ed. William Ferris. Jackson: University Press of Mississippi, 1983.

WALDVOGEL, MERIKAY. *Soft Covers for Hard Times: Quiltmaking & the Great Depression.* Nashville, Tennessee: Rutledge Hill Press, 1990.

WEBSTER, MARIE D. *Quilts: Their Story and How To Make Them.* Garden City, New York: Doubleday, Page & Co., 1915. New edition. Santa Barbara, California: Practical Patchwork, 1990.

WILSON ARTS CENTER. *Quilts Not To Sleep With.* Rochester, New York: Wilson Arts Center, The Harley School, 1988.

About the Authors

BETS RAMSEY

Bets Ramsey was born in Chattanooga, Tennessee and grew up in Oak Park, Illinois. The year she entered college her family moved back to the South. Marriage to the poet, Paul Ramsey, enabled her to live in academic communities in Minnesota, Alabama, New York, and California before returning to Tennessee in 1964. The Ramseys have four children and five grandchildren.

Mrs. Ramsey has an A. B. Degree in Art from the University of Chattanooga and a Master's Degree in Crafts from the University of Tennessee, Knoxville. She has taught art to children, college students, and adults and currently teaches Elderhostel classes at Arrowmont School of Arts and Crafts and the Appalachian Center for Crafts. She is a frequent lecturer and since 1974 has been guest curator of an annual exhibition of quilts for the Hunter Museum of Art in Chattanooga. She teaches workshops in quiltmaking and its history throughout the country.

Bets Ramsey is an active exhibiting fiber artist having shown work in more than 65 solo exhibitions and numerous group exhibitions including the Hallmark Gallery, Georg Jensen's, the New York Public Library Little Gallery, and America House in New York; the San Francisco Museum of Modern Art, the Mint Museum, the Hunter Museum, Arrowmont, and the Folger Shakespeare Library. Her work is in many private and public collections.

In 1983, with Merikay Waldvogel, Bets Ramsey began a survey of Tennessee quilts which culminated in a traveling exhibition, and a book, *The Quilts of Tennessee: Images of Domestic Life Prior to 1930*. Another book, *Old and New Quilt Patterns in the Southern Tradition*, by Bets Ramsey includes patterns of many of the quilts surveyed. For more than a decade she has written a weekly column, "The Quilter," for the *Chattanooga Times*, never running out of fascinating things to tell about quilts and quiltmaking.

She is a member and has held offices in the American Craft Council, Southern Highland Handicraft Guild, Tennessee Association of Craft Artists, Association of Visual Artists, and American Quilt Study Group, serving the Group for nine years on its Board of Directors.

GAIL ANDREWS TRECHSEL

A graduate of the College of William and Mary, Williamsburg, Virginia, Gail Andrews Trechsel first became interested in quilts as a student at the Cooperstown Graduate Program, Cooperstown, New York. Led by that interest, she wrote her thesis on the quilt collection of the New York State Historical Association in Cooperstown. Following graduate school, Gail worked at the Abby Aldrich Rockefeller Folk Art Collection in Williamsburg where she collaborated on *A Checklist of American Coverlet Weavers*. Gail worked at the Birmingham Museum of Art, Birmingham, Alabama, for nine years, first as curator of decorative arts and then assistant director. She has organized numerous exhibitions and written several museum catalogues and articles on the decorative arts. She became especially interested in Alabama-made quilts and curated *Black Belt to Hill Country: Alabama Quilts from the Helen and Robert Cargo Collection* in 1981 and wrote the accompanying catalogue.

In 1985 Gail was awarded an individual fellowship from the National Endowment for the Arts which allowed her to travel through the deep South studying Southern-made textiles. She continues to research quilt history and to visit and interview quilters, dividing her loyalty equally between traditional and studio quilts.

She and her husband, Haydn M. Trechsel, an attorney, live in Birmingham and have two children, Julia and Andrew. Their son was born while Gail was working on this book. At the age of three weeks, Andrew accompanied his mother to Chattanooga to view the first hanging of *Southern Quilts: A New View*.